GOODBYE
BUFFALO BAY

GOODBYE
BUFFALO BAY

LARRY LOYIE

WITH CONSTANCE BRISSENDEN

THEYTUS BOOKS

Library and Archives Canada Cataloguing in Publication

Loyie, Larry, 1933-
Goodbye Buffalo Bay / by Larry Loyie ; with Constance Brissenden.

ISBN 978-1-894778-62-6

I. Brissenden, Connie, 1947- II. Title.

PS8573.O979G66 2008   jC813'.6   C2008-903825-8

Printed in Canada

Credits
Cover photo of Larry Loyie courtesy of La Société Historique et Généalogique de Smoky River (Donnelly, AB). Cover photo of Buffalo Bay, Grouard, AB, courtesy of Cathy Wilcox.

www.theytus.com
In Canada: Theytus Books, Green Mountain Rd., Lot 45, RR#2, Site 50, Comp. 8
Penticton, BC, V2A 6J7, Tel: 250-493-7181
In the USA: Theytus Books, P.O. Box 2890, Oroville, Washington, 98844

 Patrimoine canadien / Canadian Heritage

We acknowledge the financial support of The Government of Canada through the Department of Canadian heritage for our publishing activities.

Canada Council for the Arts / Conseil des Arts du Canada

We acknowledge the support of the Canada Council for the Arts, which last year invested $154 million to bring the arts to Canadians throughout the country. Nous remercions le Conseil des arts du Canada de son soutien. L'an dernier, le Conseil a investi 154 millions de dollars pour mettre de l'art dans la vie des Canadiennes et des Canadiens de tout le pays.

 BRITISH COLUMBIA ARTS COUNCIL
Supported by the Province of British Columbia

We acknowledge the support of the Province of British Columbia through the British Columbia Arts Council

To all the children who attended residential school

Acknowledgements

I would like to thank the following for their support while writing this book. A grant from the Canada Council for the Arts made it possible to write and research in Alberta and British Columbia. The Aboriginal Healing Foundation has been a friend for many years. I treasure my talks with and memories of Gail Guthrie Valaskakis. Her knowledge of our shared history was invaluable. In McBride, British Columbia, Thelma (Wiltsie) Molendyk (the real Thelma) and in Vancouver, BC, Hinda Simkin (her father Sam Arbour owned the sawmill) reinforced my memories. On the theme of anger, I received insights from Karen Essex, Toronto-based psychotherapist and psychotherapy educator. Thank you to editor Jordan Wheeler and Cree translator Christine Twin. I would also like to thank James Munsey of the Alberta Railway Museum, McBride and District Public Library and local historians, Library and Archives Canada, Native Cultural Arts Museum (Grouard, Alberta), Northern Lakes College, La Société Historique et Généalogique de Smoky River, Wendy Twin, Shirley Anderson, Bob Bird, Glaslyn Library (Saskatchewan) and the great people at Theytus Books.

Contents

Part 1 – On Buffalo Bay

Part 2 – Moving On

Photographs

Part 1
On Buffalo Bay

L awrence sat on the board sidewalk watching the little boys play cowboys and Indians.

Yelling and screaming, they ran up and down the homemade wooden slide. Beneath the slide, Johnny-Johnny hid, clutching his wood chip pistol in his hand. It was the best place in the Boys Yard to find cover from his mortal enemy, Walter the Cowboy. The yard was bare except for the slide and one power pole. The only grass that grew straggled along the side of the fence that enclosed the yard.

Now that he was thirteen and a big boy at St. Bernard Mission residential school, Lawrence didn't play in the yard much. He was too busy with the other big boys like Sniffer, John, Joseph and Isaac working in the ice house or piling wood for the furnace.

When he first came to the school as a little boy of nine years old, Lawrence played on some awkward swings in the yard with wooden poles instead of rope. He tried to swing but he needed someone to push him. When the swings were torn down, they were never replaced. None of the boys missed them.

Lawrence felt the fall wind blowing. The chill in the air said that summer was coming to an end. He looked down toward Buffalo Bay and Big Prairie. The marsh grass was lush and high. Flocks of geese circled round and down into the rippling water of the huge bay. Kokom Bella would be hunting now for her evening meal and he wanted to be with her. The leaves were starting to turn yellow and red. His grandmother especially loved the red leaves.

Johnny-Johnny ran from beneath the slide and darted behind Lawrence. He spotted Walter the Cowboy hiding behind the power pole. Fast and furious, Johnny-Johnny yelled, "Bang, bang, bang!"

Walter raced toward him, pointing his finger. "Bang, you're dead," he shouted in victory. For once he was sure he had shot an Indian dead.

Swiftly, Johnny-Johnny ducked behind Lawrence. "No, I'm not," he hollered back at Walter. "You can't hit me. I'm hiding behind a big rock."

Lawrence didn't even turn his head. 'Is that all I am now, a big rock?' he thought. The funny thing was he didn't feel big at all.

Lawrence spotted Sniffer coming out of the Boys Hall. "Hey Sniffer, come and get The Hunchback of Notre Dame. I'm done with it," he called. He held up a worn copy of a Classic comic book. Sniffer walked over and sat beside Lawrence on the sidewalk. "What'cha doing?" Sniffer asked. He took a long sniff, first from the left side of his nose, then the right side. For good measure, he followed up by sniffing through both sides.

Lawrence spoke softly, even though there was nobody around to hear what he had to say. "I went to the Fathers and Brothers reading room just now. Boy, did I ever get the scare of my life."

Sniffer stopped sniffing. "What happened?" he asked eagerly.

"You know how dark and smelly that room is, with those stinky French cigarettes the priests like to smoke? I was cleaning up for them. I put some newspapers on the table and saw a picture of the lightweight champions of the world. You know, Sandy Saddler and Willie Pep. I was trying to read what it said but it was in French."

Lawrence stopped and shuddered. "What happened next?" Sniffer encouraged him.

"All of a sudden, someone was behind me. It was the priest who's not allowed to say Mass because he shakes too much. The one Brother Leblanc helps walk to the dining room to eat. I looked up at him and almost screamed. He was a giant with bulging eyes and a hunchback. He was drooling on the front of his dirty cape. He reached out like he was going to grab me. He looked just like the hunchback of Notre Dame, like the comic book picture with the black cape over his shoulders. The Fathers wear the same kind of cape, so maybe they're related."

"You got to tell the other guys," said Sniffer. "How'd you get away?"

"I ran out of there so fast." Lawrence was silent for a moment. "The funny thing is, when I got outside I felt sorry for him. I heard Brother Leblanc say he was pretty sick. He can't even speak no more. Maybe he just needed help to sit down." Lawrence shrugged and stood up. He handed Sniffer the Classic Comic. "Who's reading the comic after you? I'd like to read it again."

"It's Isaac's turn after me," said Sniffer. "It takes him a while 'cause he still don't know too much English."

High above them Sister Denise peered out the window of the Boys Hall. Her black wimple framed her small face. "Lawrence, go haul some wood into the boiler room," she shouted. "I'll send someone to help." For such a small person, Lawrence thought, her voice was loud enough to be heard in the big field at the back of the Boys Yard.

Without another word to Sniffer, Lawrence started running. "Yes, Sister," he yelled as soon as he took off. Moments later he was outside the boiler room. None of the Sisters were in sight. When he saw Barney Bottle, the wood hauler, he felt better. He knew he would have a nice talk with Barney.

"Can I pet your horses?" Like always, it was the first thing Lawrence asked.

Barney smiled a big smile. "Sure, my friend. Just hurry up so you don't get into trouble."

"I'm sure glad it's you today," Lawrence admitted. "That other guy who comes over here, the Frenchman, he's bossy and makes me do all the work."

The two horses stood patiently outside the boiler room. They tossed their heads when Lawrence came near. He stroked their foreheads, feeling the coarse hair. Then he began to carry the wood into the boiler room.

Barney finished unloading the wagon outside. He took off his work gloves and watched Lawrence work.

Lawrence heard John's "Ha ha ha" before he saw

him. John was the biggest boy in the school, taller and lankier than Lawrence. He was always laughing whether something was funny or not.

"Hello Barney," John greeted him. "I just finished delivering ice. I was on my way for a drink of water when Sister told me to come and help Lawrence."

The two boys worked quickly together. One by one, they carried the wood from the pile by the wagon. Soon they were finished.

Barney looked at his watch. "That was fast work. I just have time to unhitch and water the team and I'm done for the day."

He took a brown paper bag from his shirt pocket. "Take these. You worked hard today," he said to Lawrence. "You guys can share them with your friends."

Surprised, Lawrence stared at the gift.

"Christmas candies," Barney said. "Father Superior gave them to me. He was supposed to hand them out to the children at Christmas but he forgot. He had lots left and they were sticking together so he gave me some." He put the bag in Lawrence's hand, then jumped on his wagon and drove away to the barn.

Lawrence ran to the ice house to hide his gift.

CHAPTER 2 ~ FIVE YEARS EARLIER

When Lawrence first saw St. Bernard Mission school, he was nine years old. The buildings towered over him, dull and unfriendly. They stood in a cluster, except for the Boys Hall, a three-storey red brick building.

When the grain truck carrying the children arrived at the school, the priest was gruff. He ordered the children to jump down from the back of the truck.

Lawrence's older sister, Elizabeth, was big enough to jump on her own. Then Lawrence jumped and helped his younger sisters, Louise and Margaret.

He was helping Margaret who was scared to jump when he heard a shout.

"Get away from those girls," the priest gestured at him. "Join the boys in the line over there."

"That white man is not as kind as he was before," Margaret said softly to Lawrence.

The children stood in two lines in front of a wooden church topped with a steeple and a giant cross. Lawrence and the rest of the boys were herded toward the Boys Hall. He could see his sisters heading in a group to the Girls Hall.

Walking along, Lawrence looked down to Buffalo Bay. He didn't know where he was, only that the school overlooking the lake was far from home. The bay was beautiful in the late summer sunshine.

Above him, he saw children's faces peering out from the second-floor window of the Boys Hall. As they walked up the steps to the entrance and went inside, he heard someone say, "Charlie and Walter are back."

A harsh voice brought him back to reality. A nun stood waiting. "Hurry up you. Stop looking so dumb," she said to Lawrence. "Pay attention." Her black robes made her look like a dark cloud blotting the sky.

She addressed the boys sternly. "This will be your home for the next year. I will be addressed as Sister Denise at all times. You have a lot to do today. It will all be done before you go to bed tonight."

The Boys Hall was a large room. At the front was the Sister's desk. Around the three other sides were benches. Beneath each bench was a storage box. There were two doors on either side of the Sister's desk. These led to the refectory. When she told them about the refectory, Lawrence didn't know what she meant.

"Kîkwây eoko?" he asked the boy next to him. "What is that? What is a refectory?"

"It's the place where we eat."

Sister Denise shouted at Lawrence, "You! What is your name?"

Confused, Lawrence looked around him.

Her eyes blazing, the nun pointed at him. "You! You will not speak your heathen language in here again. If any of you savages speak your heathen language, you will be punished. Now what's your name?"

"L-L-Lawrence."

Sister Denise towered over him. Her hand came out and grabbed his hair. She gave it a yank.

"You're hurting me!"

"And what do you call me?"

"Ouch Sister," Lawrence yelped.

She pulled his hair tighter. "Never again will you answer me this way. You will always say, 'Yes, Sister' and 'No, Sister.'" She turned to the children. "Do you all understand me?"

Like a well-rehearsed chorus, the boys answered, "Yes, Sister."

"Sister, yes, Sister, yes." Lawrence stumbled over the words as if he didn't understand English at all.

Sister Denise let go of Lawrence's hair and pushed him. "Get in line and stay in line."

The boys stood in line, from smallest to tallest. Each boy was given a number. Lawrence was number twenty-six. He was put with the big boys because he was already in grade three in the public school back home.

One row of benches was piled with shirts, pants and overalls for the big boys. As they filed past, Sister Denise gave each a set of clothing: overalls, a shirt, pants and underwear.

"This will fit you," Sister Denise told Lawrence as she handed him his clothes.

She gave the middle-size boys their clothes, then the smallest boys.

They changed quickly. The big boys were already helping the little ones. Some were so young they didn't know how to dress themselves yet. The boys got back in line carrying their bundles of home clothes. They went down the stairs to a room with a wall of cubicles numbered from one to seventy.

"Remember your numbers," Sister Denise instructed them. "Every week you will change your clothes. Your washed clothes will be in your numbered box. Is that understood?"

"Yes, Sister," the boys droned like bees.

As they tramped up the stairs to the Boys Dormitory, a big boy whispered in Cree to Lawrence. "Follow the rules. If you don't do what the Sisters say you will get a beating. If you don't know what is going on, ask someone in Cree. Just don't let the little boys hear you. They will tell on you if you speak Cree. You have to speak English here."

"I can speak English pretty good," Lawrence whispered back.

After a meal of sticky gravy-like soup and a slice of bread, they played outside. The sun was still high above Buffalo Bay when Sister Denise appeared at a second-floor window. Lawrence heard a loud clapping noise.

"That's Sister's clapper. It means it's time to go in," a big boy said.

They paraded into the Boys Hall. First they took their overalls off and put them under their seat on the bench. Then they sat on the bench.

Sister Denise sat at her desk and told them what

she expected of them in the days to come. "Your parents didn't want you good-for-nothings. That's why you're here. You are here to learn about our Lord Jesus Christ, how to pray, and how to behave in church. You will learn the Mass answers in Latin and how to serve Mass. You will sing and pray in Latin and English, and you will learn to say the rosary. You will learn all of these or by the grace of God you will be punished, so help me."

It was time for bed. They washed their hands and face at the lavabo, a long row of basins. They went to the toilet. Lawrence was shown his bed in the big boys row. The first night in the Boys Dormitory was the worst of Lawrence's life. All the little boys cried in the night. Lawrence cried along with them.

Chapter 3 ~ Little Brother

Head down, hands in the prayer position, Lawrence knelt by his bed in the Boys Dormitory. At thirteen, he could recite Sister Denise's nightly lecture by heart. The only thing that had changed in five years was that his bed was now at the other end of the dormitory.

"You will sing and pray in Latin and English, and you will learn to say the rosary. You will learn all of these or by the grace of God you will be punished, so help me." With a flourish, Sister Denise picked up a container of Holy Water and strode up the first aisle.

Lawrence and the other boys who slept in the tall-ceilinged dormitory room tried hard not to wiggle on the hardwood floor. For sure if you wiggled Sister Denise would pounce on you.

The floor was cold. Lawrence felt it in his knees as Sister Denise walked up and down the aisles between the single beds, passing the bowl of Holy Water to each boy. They tipped their fingers in and then made the sign of the cross.

Afterward, Sister Denise said the final prayer. "Let us begin the Act of Contrition." She scanned the boys for signs of wiggling. Satisfied by their stillness, she continued.

"Oh, my God! I am heartily sorry for having offended Thee. I detest all my sins because I dread the loss of Heaven and the pains of Hell, but most of all because they offend Thee, my God, who art all good and deserving of all my love. I firmly resolve, with the help of Thy grace, to confess my sins, to do penance, and to amend my life."

"Amen," the boys mumbled. They crawled into their beds. Instantly, Sister Denise disappeared into her bedroom, a room on one side of the Boys Dormitory. Her small window overlooking the beds was closed.

Lawrence pulled his blankets around his chin. "She's gone," he murmured to Isaac.

"Good. I won't hear her voice 'til morning."

His new friend's face looked big against the small pillow.

Isaac wrapped his blanket more closely around himself. "It's cold in here," he shivered.

Without warning, Sister Denise opened her

window. Her floppy flannel nightcap bobbed in the frame. She looked like the Joker in a deck of cards.

"Remember boys, if you die tonight, where will you spend eternity?" Looking pleased with herself, she pulled her head back and shut her window.

"Isaac?"

His new friend gave a grunt.

"Don't forget to sleep on your right side. It gives your heart a better chance to keep beating."

Isaac's bed squeaked as he rolled over to his right side.

From a far corner of the dormitory came the soft sound of crying. Lawrence knew it was his own little brother. It was Leonard's first year in the school. He was five years old.

'Darn it! He's going to make me cry if I don't stop him,' Lawrence thought.

Sneaking to the floor he inched along the aisle keeping his head low. He knelt by Leonard's bed.

"What's the matter, little brother? Be quiet or the Sister will get you."

Leonard tried to stop a sob. "I'm lonesome for home."

"You can't keep thinking of home. Be strong. We are stuck in here and there's nothing we can do about it."

Leonard hiccupped. "The Sisters are mean to me. They call me a bad boy."

"Don't listen to them. That's how I do it."

Lawrence pulled Leonard's blanket around him and tucked him in the way Mama did.

Sister Denise poked her head out of her window. Lawrence ducked under the bed while the Sister peered around.

"I better not hear any noise out there," she said menacingly before disappearing.

"That was close." Lawrence almost mouthed the words. "Little brother, if I tell you a story, promise you'll go to sleep?"

Little brother snuggled under his blanket. "I'm ready," he said.

"One time Mama was washing clothes. You were playing on the woodpile, having fun all by yourself. Mama warned, 'Leonard, you are going to slip on the wood and hurt yourself. Go play somewhere else.'"

"I didn't want to. I was having too much fun," Leonard murmured.

"All of a sudden, you fell and let go with a yell. Mama picked you up and put you on her knee. She held you close and said sweet things to you until you fell asleep."

"I remember." Leonard smiled softly. "Is Mama in Heaven right now?"

Lawrence hesitated. The memory of his mother had made him want to cry. "Of course she is," he said in a shaky voice.

Little brother looked worried. "Mosoom Edward does not go to church. Will he go to Hell?"

"Don't be silly. Good people like Grandpa do not go to Hell." Lawrence patted Leonard gently on the head. "Go to sleep now."

Soundlessly Lawrence crawled back along the floor to his bed.

Before sleep came, Lawrence travelled home in his mind. It was a journey he made every night. Sometimes he sat and watched Mama bake a Christmas pudding. Other times he visited with Kokom on her trapline. Tonight he enjoyed his favourite memory of riding with horses and wagon to their summer camp by the river. Comforted, he fell asleep.

Chapter 4 ~ Catechism Lesson

Joseph and Isaac raced to the sidewalk and threw themselves down. Recess had just started. The sun was high and warmed the board sidewalk. If they were fast enough, they could read their comic books and maybe even trade for a new one.

Lawrence came over slowly. His eyes were red and his feet dragged. He carried a worn comic book.

"Hey you guys, my bum is sore." Lawrence sat gingerly on the sidewalk.

"How come?" Isaac asked. He looked up from his comic book. It was called A Tale of Two Cities. He didn't understand all the English words but he still liked looking at the pictures.

"I sat in the toilet last night and finished reading The Black Arrow. It was getting daylight when I got into bed."

Isaac jumped up. "Oh boy, you finished it? Now we can trade." He handed Lawrence his comic and got The Black Arrow in return.

Lawrence leaned over to look at Joseph's comic. "What comic you reading?" he asked.

Joseph pushed back his tweed cap. "It's Huckleberry Finn. It's a Classic Comic," he said.

"I like them Classic Comics. Who's after you to read it?"

"Nobody. You can have it after me. Hey, here comes Peter."

Panting slightly, Peter flopped down beside Lawrence. His skinny legs spread out over the sidewalk. "I never thought I'd get the word arithmetic in my spelling test," he blurted out.

"Why did you want arithmetic in your spelling test?" Lawrence had an easy time with spelling. The rest of the big boys knew it.

Peter sat up straight looking pleased with himself. "Because I know how to spell it. It's easy. Just remember 'A Red Indian Thought He Might Eat Tobacco in Church.' All the first letters spell arithmetic." He looked around for praise, but everyone knew it already.

Across the yard John yelled, "Come on you guys. Sister is giving turnips."

The boys ran to the side door. Sister Denise carried a dishpan full of cut turnips. One by one she gave them a small piece.

Clutching their turnips, they went back to the sidewalk. They chewed in silence. Lawrence enjoyed the juicy turnip. After potatoes and onions, it was one of his favourite foods. "I just love turnips roasted in a campfire," he said at last.

"Me too," said Joseph. "Isaac, do you ever roast turnips in the Yukon?"

Isaac shook his head. "We never eat turnips at all. We eat smoked char and moose meat. I wish I had some now."

"I think the cows eat better than we do," John said.

Lawrence was interested. "Why?" he asked.

"They get turnips every day, all sliced thin. They get cabbage and oats all chopped fine. They got fields of grass to eat whenever they're hungry."

Joseph had finished his turnip. "I wish we'd get carrots at least once," he said sadly.

"Ha ha ha ha. Oh, forget it." John stood up and nodded for his friends to follow him. "Let's go to the boiler room and practice chin-ups."

Peter jumped up eagerly. "Yeah, let's go. I don't want to be a ninety–seven–pound weakling like Charles Atlas says in the comic books." Lawrence looked around. The coast was clear. "Do we have time?" he asked.

"Sure. The Sisters have not come back to the classrooms yet."

They trooped off.

~

The schoolhouse was a white-painted two-storey wooden building. Grades one and two were in two classrooms on the main floor. On the top floor were the higher grades. Grades three and four were in one room on the top floor, and grades five to nine were in the other.

In the empty classroom, John and Lawrence sat at their desks. Lawrence drew on a scrap of paper with his pencil. John scratched away on the back of his schoolbook.

"Show me your drawing." Lawrence reached over to look at John's picture.

"It's Dick Tracy, the detective."

"Looks more like a sausage man."

"Ha ha ha ha! I guess you're right. What's yours?"

"The Phantom, the ghost who walks. He appears out of nowhere to fight crime." With a jerk, Lawrence pushed his drawing away. "This is the worst part of the morning for me," he said.

"Why don't you like it? We're gonna eat soon."

"The final thing is Catechism. Father Bighead is going to give it to us. I wonder what he's going to talk about."

"Probably something about us again."

Just then the priest bustled in dressed in his flowing black cassock. As he entered, he pulled a large white handkerchief from a deep pocket.

Lawrence groaned. "Here he comes, and smiling. He really has it in for us today."

Sister Benjamin walked to the chalkboard. As the girls and boys took their seats, Father walked over to her, turned his back to the students and spoke in French. They both chuckled.

"Just look at him smiling at the Sister," John said from the side of his mouth. "What's he telling her? Too bad we don't understand French."

Father turned to face the class. He shook his clean white handkerchief, and made a horrible noise like a rasp against metal. With a flourish, he wiped his mouth back and forth then tucked the handkerchief back in his pocket.

In a loud and dramatic voice, Father began. "Today I'll talk about the holy miracles that happened in

Europe regarding our Holy Mother, the Blessed Virgin Mary." For good measure, he took out his handkerchief again, wiped his glasses and put the handkerchief back in his pocket. He had a hard time finding the right pocket.

"He puts his hand in his pockets a hundred times a day. I wonder how many pockets he has hidden in there," Lawrence whispered.

"Maybe he has no pants under his cassock," John snickered quietly.

After a piercing glance around the classroom, Father continued. "The Holy Mother has appeared in many places but most people do not talk about it. They are afraid to be called liars or to not be believed. The most talked about ones were the sightings in Fatima and Lourdes. Three little children saw her in Fatima. Their names were Lucy, Jacinta and Francisco."

"That's a name like Frank," John whispered.

"I know that," Lawrence shot back, never taking his eyes off the priest.

"When I went back to Fatima last time, there were signs all over the place. They said do not take or disturb anything. I, of course, saw the wooden structure where the Holy Mother appeared. I reached for my pocket knife, opened it and standing on my tiptoes, I cut a little chunk of wood from the shrine."

Still smiling he rifled through his pocket and brought out a small glass container. In it was a sliver of wood.

"This comes from the shrine. See?"

He held the container high for all the class to see. The younger students gasped. Sister Benjamin beamed.

"I thought it was a sin to steal," Lawrence said under his breath.

"Maybe priests don't sin," John snorted.

Turning his head left and right, Father spotted the clock. "What! Is that the time?!"

He dug in his pocket for his watch, pulled it out and looked at it. "Ah, we just have time to say a prayer before dinner." He clasped his hands in reverence. "Boys and girls! Remember how long eternity in Hell is if you die with a mortal sin. Pray hard so that you can escape the burning fires of Hell and go to Heaven."

Lawrence studied his drawing of The Phantom as he pretended to pray.

CHAPTER 5 ~ HAIR

Isaac threw his pocket knife in the air with the flat of his hand, curving it upwards to try and make the point stick in the ground. When it hit the ground, it wobbled and fell over.

"Darn it," he said. The big boys sitting in the circle ignored him. They had their marbles out and were counting them on the ground.

"Hey guys, let's play Knife," Isaac begged.

Not a glance from the other boys.

Lawrence liked the look of his blue marbles. He had two of them. They were as clear as the sky on a sunny day.

Keechee lined up his marbles and counted them. He had fifteen in all. "No sneaking is a good thing when you're playing marbles," he said. Keechee was the best marble player around. Because he had a bad leg, he couldn't play many other games. He didn't want to lose any of his marbles to someone who was cheating.

"I like the No Cleaning rule. Nobody should brush away the stones," John said.

Joseph jumped up. "Gee willigers, I gotta go to the toilet," he said. He ran off.

"Let's play Knife," Isaac repeated. He stood up and threw his pocket knife from a standing position. "I can do it better this way," he said to no one in particular.

Panting, Joseph ran back to the group.

"Back so soon?" Lawrence was surprised.

Joseph twitched with excitement. "Sniffer's in the toilet throwing up his guts. He's got his whole arm down his throat, right down to his belly."

"What's he doing that for?"

"He thinks he swallowed some hair. His eyes look like a chicken's behind. Somebody told him that Marcel swallowed some hair and it swelled up in his stomach, and that's what killed him."

"Is that why Freddie is making that noise?" Lawrence gagged like someone throwing up.

"Ha ha ha, they're harmonizing in two toilets," John said.

Joseph turned to Lawrence. "You saw Marcel. Do you think he was dead?"

Lawrence scratched his head. "I went to the toilet

upstairs in the dormitory. Marcel was upstairs sick in bed and I walked right by him. He was staring at the ceiling not moving, just like he was dead."

Joseph shuddered. "Don't be silly, your eyes close when you die. You never see them bury a guy with his eyes open."

"All I know is what I saw when I came out of the toilet. Marcel was still staring at the ceiling. The back of my hair stood up. I did not look back, I just ran down the stairs, that's how scared I was."

Sniffer staggered over. His pockets were weighed down with marbles and his school pants hung low.

Isaac forgot about Knife. "Hey, Sniffer, did you reach your stomach and get all the hair you swallowed?"

Sniffer groaned. "Gosh my belly hurts."

"It should. Between you and Freddie, you've been at it all morning. Are you that scared to die or something?"

"You know you're going to lose your pants, with all them marbles you carry," said Lawrence.

Sniffer wiped his nose on his sleeve. "Naw, I got a piece of rope I can use as a belt." He held up a piece of rope and his pants fell down. He was wearing baggy undershorts. The boys burst out laughing.

The school bell rang. Like mist, they disappeared

in a run to the school.

Clutching his pants, Sniffer chased after them.

Chapter 6 ~ Sister Theresa

How's my little brother Perry? How's he doing?" Hazel's brown eyes flashed at Lawrence. He stopped inside the entrance of the school to answer her. 'The big girls from the Yukon are beautiful,' he thought. He tried not to stare. Her friend Joyce stood beside Hazel, watching curiously, her curly hair framing her impish face.

"He's staying out of trouble. The little boys help each other. He can speak some Cree now."

"I don't see him much, being on the other side of the yard," Hazel said.

"Kimiyosin," Lawrence said. He knew she wouldn't understand what he'd said—"You're beautiful"— because she didn't speak Cree.

Hazel frowned. "What are you saying? Are you teasing me?"

Joyce giggled and pushed Hazel toward Lawrence. His arms reached out to stop her from falling. He could feel the softness of her body as he steadied her.

"What are you doing here?"

The threesome froze.

The grade two teacher stood by her classroom door. "Wait here," she said. In a minute she was back. She handed Lawrence a note. "Give this to Sister Theresa. You are going to stay after school all week and help her." She turned to Hazel. "Get back into your classroom. You are supposed to be helping with the grade one children."

Looking down at the floor, Joyce hid her face beneath her hair. The teacher handed her a note.

"And you. Take this to Sister Benigna. I recommend that both of you stay after school for a week."

Lawrence took his note to Sister Theresa, the high school teacher. She was tall with clear blue eyes that reminded him of his marbles. Most of the time he had ignored her, like he did the other Sisters.

Sister Theresa took the note and read it quickly. "What happened?" she asked.

He told her how it happened. For a moment, he thought she was going to laugh.

"That's a good story," she said.

"It's not a story. It's the truth."

"I believe you." Sister Theresa smiled gently. Her smile made him feel special.

The third day he stayed after school, Sister Theresa said, "If you don't want to stay and help me, you can leave."

She was giving him a break, Lawrence knew. The truth was he didn't want to stop coming to her classroom after school. It was a strange place to find a kind person who also wanted to teach you. She talked to him like he was a person, not just number twenty-six.

"I'll stay," Lawrence said.

Sister Theresa sat at her desk. She gestured to him to sit down. "What would you really like to learn before your holidays?" she asked.

The question startled him. The first thing that came to his mind was to play the piano. He told her this shyly, afraid she would laugh.

"Is there anything else you'd like to learn?"

"Typing." 'Where did that come from?' Lawrence questioned himself. It was too late to take it back. Anyway, it was true. In the movies, they showed reporters typing, like Clark Kent, the Superman. It looked good to him.

Sister Theresa looked at him seriously. "You would make a good student if you worked at it. Studying can be fun and reading is the secret for good grades."

On her desk was a globe of the world. She pushed it toward him. "Spin it," she told him. "Take this pencil. Close your eyes and when the globe stops, point to a place anywhere in the world."

With a push he spun it around fast. He closed his eyes and pointed. The pencil landed on Africa.

"Have you been to Africa?" he asked, his eyes wide. He had read about lions in Africa.

"You have picked a place that I have never been. But we can still talk about it. That's what learning is all about."

"Do they have moose in Africa?"

Sister Theresa shook her head. "No, but I think you know a lot about the animals around here. Why don't we compare the animals you know with the ones in Africa?"

"I've never been to Africa."

"You never know, you may go there one day. Try to travel when you grow up. See as many countries as you can. Learn about the people, their cultures and national events."

Week after week, Lawrence stayed behind to help Sister Theresa. He liked going to the classroom. Mostly, he enjoyed his time with her.

Now he was learning.

Chapter 7 ~ The Secret

The smell of stale tobacco smoke made Lawrence's nose wrinkle. The priests' reading room was scattered with spittoons full of spit from snuff and chewing tobacco. The new Dutch priest smoked black tobacco that looked like tiny black roots. Lawrence had seen him skating on Buffalo Bay wearing his cassock and fancy ice skates strapped on his shoes. No one was in the room that afternoon. They were having an afternoon nap.

He passed through the reading room and slipped into the travelling priest's room. Today Father Letourneau was in Peavine, a couple of hours away. Lawrence liked his sermons on Sundays. They were funny and always made people laugh.

Lawrence knew where to look for the gun. It was in the bottom drawer of Father's dresser, John had said. He pulled it open. The gun lay on the top of Father's socks. He picked it up, put it in his overall pocket and left as quietly as he had entered.

The ice house was empty when he got there. Lawrence closed the door behind him. No one had seen him go in. The ice was hauled from Buffalo Bay with horse and sleigh, load after load, until the ice house was filled with ice blocks. Then they were covered with sawdust to keep from melting. The ice cooled all the ice boxes in the Mission. The interior was crowded, cool and peaceful.

Lawrence was sorry that John wasn't in the ice house to share his secret. 'I'll wait here to show the guys,' he thought. 'They'll be along soon.' It was their favourite place to meet without being seen by Sister Denise. She would never go to the ice house.

He took the gun out of his pocket. For such a small object, it was heavy. His .22 back home didn't seem to weigh as much. He could easily carry it under his arm when he went hunting for rabbits.

He wished the guys would hurry up. If he didn't get the gun back soon, Father Letourneau might come back for dinner. Then he might open his drawer and find the gun missing. Lawrence couldn't imagine what would happen then. 'I guess I'd just keep the gun. I'd hide it somewhere,' he made his mind up.

Lawrence relaxed. 'Father might not come back at all. Maybe he'd eat in a café tonight?'

He raised the gun. It wasn't the kind The Phantom carried. More like a gangster gun. He stared at a big block of ice, the gun pointing. "I'll show you guys I'm tough," he scowled.

Bang! The gun went off.

Lawrence froze. Somebody was sure to come running. He'd had it now. He waited, listening for footsteps.

No one came.

He opened the door and slipped out of the ice house, walked across the churchyard and into the priests' residence. He went up the stairs and slipped the gun back in the drawer. No one saw him. No one knew. 'Lucky this time,' he thought.

CHAPTER 8 ～ CHRISTMAS

A lone figure shovelled snow on the enormous skating rink. The sun had set long before in the early winter night.

One shovel of snow, then another was heaved to the side of the rink. It was cold but Lawrence didn't feel it. Head down, arms lifting, he was intent on clearing the snow off the rink. Panting, he finally stopped with almost all the rink clear.

'I'll do the rest tomorrow after we practise for the Christmas concert,' he told himself. When he had started shovelling the snow a week ago, it was up to his knees. First he had cleared a figure eight in the middle of the rink, his and his alone to practise on. He skated forward, then backward around the figure eight until he could skate in either direction without thinking. Sometimes he added a twirl just to look fancy. If he didn't fall, he felt good.

He hoisted the shovel over his shoulder and stood and looked over his work. The ice glowed under the yard lights. Tomorrow he would finish. Then he could skate all he wanted.

As he walked into the Boys Hall, John and Joseph were shaking their mops outside.

"You better hurry," Joseph said. "The Sister has something to tell us."

Inside the Boys Hall, Sister Denise was busy sewing. The boys sat quietly talking to each other. When the floor was being mopped, they had to stay seated.

Sister Denise stood up when she saw the three boys enter. "Is the mopping finished?" she asked.

"Yes, Sister," they said in unison. They sat down on their bench seats.

Sister Denise clapped her clapper. The boys stared at her, anxious to hear the news. "The good Father Superior has decided that all the boys and girls are going down to Buffalo Bay tomorrow for a walk and to skate. You will have hot cocoa when you are finished playing," she announced.

A ripple of excitement went through the Boys Hall. The boys couldn't believe their luck. They never went out of the Boys Yard except to pick potatoes or pile wood. The girls would be there too. They never played with the girls. They weren't allowed to talk to them, not even their sisters. And hot cocoa. The anticipation of hot cocoa made their mouths water.

Lawrence had watched the girls walking back and forth from the Girls Hall to the outside toilets. They always walked in pairs or threes. He wondered what they talked about. Did they ever get tired of walking back and forth?

None of the boys slept well that night. Their voices rose and fell until Sister opened the window and threatened to cancel the outing unless they went to sleep. After that, all was silent.

~

Buffalo Bay stretched white across to Big Prairie. Patches of snow covered the ice here and there where the wind could not blow it off.

A parade made its way down the hill to the bay. The boys went first, carrying skates and hockey sticks they had made in Brother Nicol's carpentry shop. The girls followed, their colourful hats bobbing. Brother Nicol walked with them. The children were happy to have the Brother along. He was kind, with an encouraging word for everyone. As usual, he carried his camera.

When they reached the frozen expanse of Buffalo Bay, Lawrence bent over to put on his school skates. They were brown and battered, worn by many boys before him. They were patched up but comfortable on his feet.

Looking up he saw Jocelyn, a big girl, standing next to him. She held out a pair of shiny new skates. "Want to borrow my speed skates?" Jocelyn asked. "All the girls watched you cleaning the rink this week. You're a good skater. My skates will go good on the rink."

Lawrence's eyes widened. The skates were something like the Dutch priest wore, with long slim blades. "Don't you want to sk-skate?" he stuttered.

Jocelyn's face turned pink. "I'm not that good at skating."

Lawrence slipped on the speed skates and tied them up. They fit perfectly. He pushed off, getting the feel of them. He had to keep the fronts up or he would trip. He moved his feet sideways like the Dutch priest. He went faster, flying along the ice. Before he knew it he was far out on Buffalo Bay.

The cold winter air shot through his lungs in wild, fresh breaths. He could see clearly across the bay to Big Prairie. 'I could skate home,' he told himself. 'No one could catch me.'

Lessons from his grandfather flooded his mind. "You don't go out alone in winter unless you have everything you need to survive," Mosoom had warned him. 'Maybe next time,' Lawrence reconsidered. Besides, if he took off, he'd miss the hot cocoa.

He could barely hear the children who were skating close to the shore. Reluctantly, he slowed down and circled around. The children were running to the Sisters to get their cup of cocoa. In no time he was back with them, sipping the special once-in-five-years drink.

~

Silent Night filled the Boys Hall. Sister Benjamin was playing the piano. She kept a close eye on the boys and girls standing in rows in front of her. The night of the Christmas concert was only a week away.

The children blew into their red kazoos, humming Silent Night along with the piano. Some of the children didn't know the hymn, but they hummed loudly anyway.

The kazoo was new to Lawrence. It wasn't like

the fiddles and guitars he loved back home. But it was music and he was good at music. He blew into his kazoo with all his might. His lips tickled when he blew. 'At least I know the tune,' he thought. 'I could sing Silent Night all by myself.'

Besides, there were girls blowing away on their kazoos. Jocelyn winked at him when Sister Benjamin wasn't looking.

"You're out of tune," Lawrence elbowed Isaac.

"My lips are itchy." Isaac rubbed his lips furiously with his hand. "I hate that feeling."

After the kazoo, they practised singing songs in Latin. The children sang high and Lawrence sang low.

"Someone here is harmonizing." Sister Benjamin scrutinized the children. "Adeste Fidelis is not a song; it's a hymn. There will be no harmonizing."

"But it sounds good," Isaac said under his breath.

The entire village of Grouard was invited to the concert. The Boys Hall was decorated with crepe paper and red paper bells. The families crowded in. Some of their children were ex-terns, students who attended the school during the day and went home at night.

The smaller children acted the Nativity scene

wearing costumes sewn by the big girls and the Sisters. Then all the children sang Silent Night on their kazoos to great applause.

When it was the big children's turn, Lawrence sang like he did back home. The children sang high and he sang low, harmonizing Adeste Fidelis.

Chapter 9 ~ The Hospital

Lawrence lay in his bed alone in the Boys Dormitory. Sometimes his body was freezing, at other times burning hot. He was glad he had asked Sister Gabriel for a pitcher of water. When he was able, he sat up and drank from a cup.

He smelled smoke and heard voices outside. He felt his bed being pushed to a corner room at the far end of the dormitory. Then he was alone again. He could see smoke slipping in under the bottom of the door.

He did not care. He had already planned his escape. 'First I'll climb out the window. Then slide down the roof over the steam bath. I'll drop on the ground and into the boiler room.' He hoped he would be strong enough to do it.

The smoke seemed everywhere now. He was too sick to care. Before he had the strength to take a drink, he drifted off to sleep.

"Ad Deum qui laetificat..." Father Fatso was

kneeling by his bed, speaking in Latin. 'What's he doing here,' Lawrence thought. 'I don't like him.'

When he woke next, he thought Sister Theresa was holding his hand. Her touch was soft and warm.

~

The room where he woke up was unfamiliar. Someone came in. A night light went on. A woman in a white uniform stood beside his bed.

"Am I dead?" Lawrence asked. "Is this Heaven?"

The nurse laughed. "You're not dead. You're in the hospital."

She picked up a glass of water. "Have a sip of this. You are a lucky boy. Your temperature was one hundred and five. We almost lost you."

It was difficult to walk but the nurse helped him take a few steps. Dr. Wood came in and checked him over. After a week the doctor told him, "You're doing much better. But we'll keep you here a little longer just to be sure."

It was good to be away from the Mission school. The nurse took him to the lounge and showed him a pile of magazines. He chose the biggest one from the pile. It said Look on the cover with a colour photo of a man waving a red cape at a bull. It reminded him of the time he went raspberry picking with Papa and his sisters. When Rainy Hall's herd of wild cows came by, the children ran and climbed a tree. Papa went on picking with the fearsome cows all around him, as if they weren't even there.

A man named Ernest Hemingway wrote the story in the magazine. He lived in Spain where it was hot and where bullfighters fought fierce bulls. In a photograph, Hemingway and some pretty ladies watched a bullfight from the stands. The magazine had more pictures of mountains and rivers.

'I want to be a writer,' Lawrence vowed. He thought of Sister Theresa and her geography lessons. 'I'm going to travel to faraway countries,' he promised himself. 'Just like Hemingway the writer.'

~

A light snow was falling. Although it was spring, a cold wind blew across Buffalo Bay. For no special reason Lawrence went into the classroom early. Sister Theresa stood at her desk.

"Lawrence, please come over here. I have something to tell you." She waited until he reached her desk. "I'm leaving the school soon. I've been transferred to Yakima, Washington," Sister Theresa said.

Tears sprang to Lawrence's eyes. He held them back.

"Why do you have to go?" The words came out raw and hurting.

Sister Theresa walked around the desk and put her hand on his shoulder. "There's nothing I can do about it. I have to go where I'm told. I'm going to miss my students here. Most of all I will miss you, Lawrence. You are so eager to learn now. I hope you won't give up when I'm gone."

The tears that Lawrence had held back ran freely now. Sister Theresa took a handkerchief out of her pocket and handed it to him. She said nothing while he wiped his eyes, knowing his hurt and disappointment.

After he stopped crying she said, "There is one thing you can do for me. I want you to promise you will keep on reading. Read, read and read some more."

Later that day, Lawrence stood at a second-floor window and watched Sister Theresa get into the black car that would take her away across

Buffalo Bay and into the world. When he studied with her, he was somebody. He was never going to let that go.

Chapter 10 ~ Jackie

Laughter floated out of the Boys Hall. All the boys were gathered there, waiting for Sister Denise. Lawrence hurried to wash up and join them before the Sister arrived.

He spotted Sniffer, John and Isaac sitting on a bench reading comic books. Lawrence shoved them over and squeezed himself on the bench beside them.

A hush fell over the room at the sound of Sister Denise. She entered, her black robes flapping. With one hand she dragged a little boy by the hair. A cold shiver ran through Lawrence. The little boy was his cousin Jackie. It was his cousin's first year at the school. He was a tough little guy of six years old. Not a whimper or a cry came from his mouth.

The other boys looked at the floor, looked at the ceiling, looked at their hands. They looked everywhere but not at Sister Denise and Jackie.

Sweat poured from under Sister Denise's

wimple. She shouted at Jackie, half in French and half in English. "Mon gros sauvage d'Indien. Who do you think you are, Jackie, King of the Bush? You good-for-nothing. Are you even too dumb to cry?"

Sister Denise shoved her thumb into Jackie's mouth. Holding his head with both hands she shook him vigorously.

'Cry, scream or bawl,' Lawrence begged Jackie wordlessly. 'All you have to do is make a noise and she will let you go.' Still Jackie did not cry out.

Sister Denise's face was bright red. With a powerful yank, she dragged Jackie down to the floor. One, two, three, she pounded his head on the cement floor.

"Say something, Jackie, you gros salud. All you do is eat, sleep and go to the toilet. No wonder you don't know nothing," she shrieked.

The boy in her hands went limp. Eyes blazing, Sister Denise let go of his head, leaving him lying on the floor.

Lawrence, looking fearfully from the corner of his eye, watched as Sister Denise took a dozen deep breaths. She pulled her shoulders back. Looking at no one she rearranged her habit, smoothing down the black robe and straightening the rosary beads that hung from her belt. Casting her eyes around at the boys, she took her clapper out of her pocket. She banged it twice, making a loud snapping noise.

Her voice quivered when she spoke. "Sit down, all of you. You wild devils, you will learn your lessons. It's no wonder you don't know nothing running around the bush like wild animals." She strode around the room. She did not even glance at Jackie who lay passed out on the floor. Lawrence felt sick looking at his cousin. He wanted to cry out, to scream, to jump up and punch her, but he was too afraid to make a move.

Sister Denise turned swiftly and headed toward the stairwell. Stopping by the door she turned back again. "Lawrence, take Isaac with you and mop the floor. Make sure he does it right or you'll both be punished. People like him from the Yukon don't know how to clean a floor. The rest of you get ready for bed."

Sister Denise disappeared. When they were sure she was gone, Sniffer and John picked Jackie up and carried him to his bench. He lay sprawled out on the bench as if he was sleeping.

Lawrence and Isaac went to the broom closet and took out two mops. Starting on opposite sides of the room, they mopped the Boys Hall floor, up and down, up and down. They didn't speak. Lawrence thought of Jackie and the sound of his head hitting the floor with a bang. He wanted to throw up.

Isaac spoke in a soft voice. At first when Isaac came to the school, he only spoke Tlingit. After a month he had picked up some English and Cree and began to make friends.

"What's the matter with you? You don't look too good," Isaac said.

"I'm going to run away."

Isaac stopped mopping. His mouth dropped. "You what?"

"You heard me right. I'm going to run away. I have to get out of here."

"How would you get home?"

"I'm not going home. Maybe I'll go to Texas like in the cowboy movies. They got mountains in Texas. I want to see them."

"We got mountains in the Yukon, too. The tops are covered with snow most of the time." Isaac made his mind up. "I'm gonna come too," he said.

Lawrence hesitated before he spoke. "My biggest worry is crossing the bridge. You know it's a mile long."

Isaac frowned. "If Father Superior is driving on the bridge we'll get caught for sure."

"I'll run it," Lawrence said. He bit his lower lip. "It'd be worth a beating to get out of here even for a while."

The floor was finished. The polished cement gleamed under the lights. Lawrence gathered up the mops. "Let's you and me talk about it some more tomorrow. Okay?"

Isaac nodded and they headed off for bed.

Chapter 11 ~ Little Boats

The two friends, Lawrence and Isaac, stood outside the boys' toilets at recess, watching the little boys playing in the thawing snow. Little brother Leonard set his homemade boat in a stream and pushed it along with a stick. His boat was just a small piece of wood.

"Look at the little boys having fun playing in the puddles," said Isaac. "I used to do that."

"Look at Leonard watching his make-believe sailboat disappear. He doesn't even know if it would make it all the way to the bay or not." Lawrence kicked a piece of melting snow, sending it flying. 'It's like their make-believe sailboats are carrying their sadness away with them,' he thought.

Isaac stomped a clod of dirty snow into mush. "It sure is nice in spring, snow thawing, water running all over the place."

"Yeah. All running down to the bay."

"It's got to run to the coulee first," Isaac said.

"I know that," Lawrence said impatiently.

The school bell rang from the second-floor window. Recess was over.

"Darn it, why can't they let the little kids play longer. Just look at the fun they're having."

Isaac heard the anger in Lawrence's voice. He nodded in agreement. "It's like a crime for them to enjoy themselves. Bastards," Isaac said.

One of the little boys rushed past them. They watched him hustle by, a desperate look on his face. Isaac laughed. "Look at Billy, he forgot to go to the toilet. Look at him holding his thing. He'll never make it. It's a spanking for him now."

Lawrence couldn't help but laugh too. "Not if his pants dry before dinner."

"I think he's going to make it."

"He made it!"

They walked toward the schoolhouse.

"Isaac, I'm going today, after lunch, at high noon. When they think I'm in the ice house working."

"We can run together." They were almost at the steps of the school. "See you later then," Isaac said to Lawrence.

They parted company going into their separate classrooms.

~

Getting to the bridge was easy because the boys were hidden by bushes all the way. At the foot of the bridge, they stopped, under cover of a willow bush. The bridge was long and narrow crossing over Buffalo Bay. If two cars met on the bridge, one had to move into a pullover while the other passed by.

"If anyone comes, we'll go over the side of the bridge and hide," Lawrence said. "It's a mile long but we can make it."

"What if Father Superior catches us?" Isaac asked.

"The bridge is the worst part. Once we get across, we're free." Lawrence took a deep breath and began to run. His legs were strong from skating all winter.

At first Isaac kept up. After a time his breath came heavier and faster. He started to fall behind. Lawrence slowed down to let his friend catch up.

The wind behind them pushed them on until at last they could see the end of the bridge. Lawrence felt the thrill of freedom. He could run forever if he had to.

They made it to the other side and turned off the bridge. Panting, they stopped to rest in the willow bushes. Isaac was breathing heavily, but he soon caught his breath. They sipped a handful of cool water from Buffalo Bay.

"Let's shortcut across the open field. We'll get away from here faster," Lawrence said. Isaac nodded.

As they started across the field, they saw the black car on the highway. They ran faster. The car slowed down and pulled over. Father Superior stepped out.

"Stop right there, boys. You have no place to go," he yelled after them.

Lawrence and Isaac ran on.

"We'll get the police after you," Father Superior threatened.

The two boys stopped running. Standing in the middle of the endless prairie, they looked at each other.

"Let's go back," Isaac said.

Lawrence shrugged. "I'm hungry anyway," he said. They trudged back to the road.

Father Superior had the car door open. He shoved Isaac into the back seat. With a swift move, he grabbed Lawrence by the hair and hit him in the body with a clenched fist.

Lawrence had never been hit by a man before. His mouth opened in disbelief as the pain vibrated through his body. He fell on top of Isaac, gasping for breath. Afraid for himself, Isaac did not look at Lawrence. The car began to move back to the school.

CHAPTER 12 ~ GOODBYES

The big boys stood around the Boys Yard, talking in the spring sunshine.

"Who's your favourite cowboy?" Joseph asked Lawrence. "I like Lash LaRue with his whip. He reminds me of Sister Denise."

"I like Randolph Scott. He's a good fighter."

"I wonder if them cowboys get hurt when they get hit like that?" Isaac asked, looking puzzled.

Lawrence shook his head. "It's just pretending," he said. "My sister Elizabeth told me. She reads romance and movie magazines. That's all she reads at home. She knows everything about them actors."

Joseph jumped around Lawrence, his fists in the air. "Let's make-believe we're fighting. I'll be the good guy and you be the bad guy."

Lawrence stepped back and raised his fists. "I'll swing my fist to your face. When it gets close to your chin, turn sideways. It will look like I really socked you."

"I'll stagger back to the fence and bang against it." Joseph showed how he would do it.

"Okay, let's go."

From her window, Sister Denise looked down on the fighting. She hollered, "Lawrence, gros sauvage, get in here."

"Dammit, what did I do now?" Lawrence said under his breath.

He paced toward the Boys Hall. He thought of all the beatings, getting hit with her big ring of keys, the lies she told about his family and being punished for things he didn't do. She beat Jackie until his face was not right. How many other boys did she do this to?

As he climbed the stairs to the second floor he thought of Sister Denise's hateful face. 'This is it. I was good before I got here. At least when somebody calls me a Mission Bean, I'm something. Here, I'm nothing. One thing I know, you will never hit me again,' he promised.

He saw Keechee sitting on a bench in the Boys Hall. Lawrence ignored him. He was angrier than he had ever been. His fists were clenched as he came into the Boys Hall. As he walked toward Sister Denise, he tried to unclench them. But they stayed in hard balls.

Sister Denise's eyes blazed. Then she saw his fists. Suddenly, Lawrence saw fear in her eyes.

"Why were you fighting?" Her voice was sharp.

"We weren't fighting. We were playing."

Sister Denise raised her hand to grab his hair. Lawrence glared at her. His anger almost made him cry. He took a step forward, his fists by his side, clenching and unclenching them.

"You ain't never gonna hit me again," he said in a voice as sharp as hers.

Sister Denise backed away. "Go and play outside," she said shakily. She walked over to her window in the corner, her face turned away from Lawrence.

Lawrence looked at Keechee sitting on the bench. Still angry, Lawrence spoke in Cree, "Tânehki ekâ ka-wîmetawen marbles wayawîtimihk." Keechee said nothing. In English, Lawrence asked the same question, "Why aren't you playing marbles outside?"

"My leg is sore," Keechee whispered in English. He didn't look up. If the Sister heard him talking to Lawrence, he'd get a punishment for sure. Lawrence was sorry he had put Keechee on the spot.

He turned and walked to the door leading to the stairs. Isaac was waiting at the top of the stairwell, smiling. Lawrence took a deep breath as if he hadn't breathed for a long time. He tried to smile but it felt crooked on his face.

"I've been wanting to do that since Jackie got beat up," Lawrence said.

"You really did it. I heard you. And Sister didn't hit you." Isaac grinned. Then a shadow crossed his face. "I wonder if she'll try to hit you again?"

"She won't. Because I meant it."

They walked down the stairs together.

"I've got to go to the toilet," he told his friend. He wanted to be alone. He went to his favourite spot by the slide and sat down. The sun warmed his face. Quiet was all around him. Shaking his head he realized no one was playing near him. No one called out to him. 'It's like I have the plague,' he realized, 'now that I stood up to Sister Denise. Just like Keechee, they're all afraid to talk to me.'

A wave of guilt washed over him. 'Why is it that I always feel guilty?' he thought. 'The little ones don't seem to mind this place. If they behave and do what they're told, they're fine. Was I like that when I first came? Did I try that hard to follow the rules?'

He had stood up to Sister Denise. Still, he felt fear, this time about himself. His anger was powerful but frightening. He had won, but what was it he had won?

~

The grain truck was parked by the church ready to take the children home for the summer.

Lawrence looked around for Isaac. He couldn't see his friend anywhere. In his heart, Lawrence didn't want to say goodbye to Isaac. 'This is it,' Lawrence thought. 'I'll be fourteen in the fall. I won't be coming back. I'm going home for good. I should be happy.'

Somehow, it was as hard to leave as it was to arrive almost five years before. Some boys were laughing and playing as they waited to go home. Others stood in tears knowing they were staying behind. There was nothing he could do about them and it hurt to see them.

Isaac came out from behind the ice house. It was his last day, too. He was going home to the Yukon. They sat on the sidewalk talking.

"Maybe I'll make it to the Yukon one day," said Lawrence.

"If you do, look me up. If I ever come down your way, I'll ask around for you," Isaac said.

"One day we'll meet up. Maybe we'll run away together again."

They laughed.

"That was stupid, wasn't it?" said Isaac.

"No, it wasn't. We finally did something we wanted to do. It didn't matter if we got beat up for it. It was worth it just to get away for a while."

With trembling voices they said goodbye.

Lawrence climbed onto the back of the grain truck. He was finally tall enough to pull himself up and peer over the side.

As the truck pulled out of the schoolyard, he forgot about Isaac. He was going home.

Part 2
Moving On

Chapter 13 ~ Rabbit Hill

The grain truck pulled up in front of the church in the town of Slave Lake. When the back doors opened, Lawrence saw his older sister, Elizabeth, waiting. She was wearing a colourful print dress and had a grown-up air about her.

Lawrence was the last to climb down, after his younger sisters, Margaret, Louise and Alberta and little brothers, Leonard and Buddy. They stood in a group beside the truck, hugging Elizabeth.

"Papa couldn't make it," she explained. "He's repairing pack saddles for Mr. Eben on the north shore of the lake. Mr. Eben is trying to find a man for his pack trip tomorrow. If he can't, Papa will have to go and he won't be home for two weeks."

They started toward Rabbit Hill. "While we're walking home, you can tell me your stories," Elizabeth told the younger children. "I know you have a lot to tell. I made you supper. Kokom Bella is watching it for me until we get back."

"I'll run ahead," Lawrence said. He soon reached the familiar turn off the highway and ran up Rabbit Hill. Near the top, he spotted their log house in the distance. His grandmother was nowhere to be seen. At the front door, he stopped and paused. The smell of Elizabeth's fresh-baked bread floated out and made him think of Mama.

He knew what was inside, the kitchen with the cook stove, wooden table and chairs, and a cupboard for dishes and pots and pans. There was a stand for water buckets. In the front room in winter, there was a big airtight heater but now it was summer and it would be stored in the shed. Three small bedrooms were off the front room.

He knew what was not inside. Mama was not there. He didn't want to think how she had died two years ago while he was at the Mission school. He wasn't at home, he never saw her dead. Maybe she had just gone away and would come back one day. Even though he knew it wasn't true, he still wished for it.

With a start, he saw his grandmother was standing beside him. "Nosîsim," she said. "My grandson." She was smaller than he remembered but her hug was strong and the sound of her Cree was comforting.

They entered the log house together.

~

Papa didn't come home the next day. The children were by themselves.

Lawrence watched his brothers and sisters playing tag in the yard. Chasing each other, they laughed and shouted. Their laughter sounded beautiful, something he'd never noticed before. They were free of worries for the summer. Come September, they would go back to the Mission school. The truck would come and they would climb on. This time, he wouldn't be with them. A gnawing feeling gripped his heart.

His old bicycle leaned against the logs. Testing it out, it was as good as ever. "Want to ride?" he yelled at the children. They crowded around him. Now that he was bigger, he could ride two of them, one on the seat and one on the handlebars. Leonard and Buddy climbed on.

Lawrence peddled down the forestry trail. Everything at home was the same, yet it felt strange and different. He was finally free. What did freedom mean? It was always on his mind. When the other children went back, what was he going to do? What if he was forced to go back to the school? He vowed he never would.

~

The next day, Lawrence rode his bicycle down Rabbit Hill to town. 'What am I going to do?' he thought over and over as he peddled on the gravel highway. 'I have to find a job. But what can I do?'

Town was a small place, with a post office and two general stores. The few blocks were filled up with two garages and a pool hall, two cafés and a legion hall where movies were shown on Saturday night.

He pulled up in front of the post office and jumped off his bicycle. A light rain had fallen, just enough to keep the dust down. People walked along the board sidewalks. Turning, he almost bumped into Uncle Dave. A smile cracked Lawrence's face when he saw his uncle. He started to say something, then pulled back.

Uncle Dave was staring at him with a puzzled look. He said nothing and walked on.

Lawrence watched Uncle Dave walk away. He wanted to run after him and say, "How are you,

Uncle?" Nothing came out of his mouth. 'Why didn't I greet him like I wanted to,' Lawrence questioned himself. 'I should have told him who I was, but I didn't say anything. How was he supposed to know me? I'm the stranger now, not him,' he thought miserably.

Nothing would ever be the same again, he was convinced. He was too afraid to talk to older people anymore. After so many years in the residential school, he wasn't used to it. He never spoke to any adults at the Mission except the workers. And only some of them, like Barney Bottle, were kind and helpful.

Lawrence was invisible, like The Phantom. No one seemed to know him anymore.

P eople came from all over the country to the small town of Kinuso for the rodeo and sports days. Like always, they started on July first and ran until the third. The rodeo grounds were full of activities. Events like wild bronco riding and bull riding were packed with onlookers.

Around the grounds, vendors and spectators bustled about. Some were putting up tents wherever they could find a space. Others greeted old friends.

Lawrence strutted around, wearing his Cowboy King jeans. Papa had surprised him by leaving him money to buy new clothes. He felt proud of his new jeans and his blue plaid shirt with snap buttons. He laughed to himself, remembering the time when he and Elizabeth were caught opening the Christmas presents Mama had hidden in a trunk. He had tried on his new red shorts and was wearing them when Mama walked in. He got a slap on the bum that time.

Most everyone else at the rodeo was wearing

white cowboy shirts. A few sported buckskin jackets and cowboy boots. White shirts to Lawrence meant wearing a suit, thanks to his sister Elizabeth and her favourite movie magazines. Blue was his favourite colour.

In an out-of-the-way corner, he watched a group of Cree men playing bone games. They sat in two rows facing each other. One of the players was a huge man. While the drummers sang and played, the man weaved his hands back and forth trying to confuse his opponents. He hid the bone in his left hand, then his right and sometimes even in both hands.

"Give it up, Muxseem," a laughing man on the other team cried out, pointing to the big man's left hand. Muxseem handed the bones over and the game continued.

Lawrence left the players and wandered back to the rodeo grounds. Over by a corral, he saw his Uncle Louis wearing leather chaps that protected a rider's legs when he was competing. Lawrence knew Uncle Louis was the best hunter around. He was surprised to learn that he was also a cowboy.

"Are you riding today?" he asked his uncle shyly.

"I have to ride pretty soon," Uncle Louis said. "Not sure when. Why don't you go and find Mosoom?

Your grandfather has a tent over there by the edge of the trees. He wants to see you."

It was easy to find Mosoom Edward's white canvas tent. Lawrence stepped inside. Grandfather was sitting on the ground on his bear rug.

"Kayâs, Mosoom." The Cree greeting came naturally to Lawrence. Seeing his grandfather's familiar kindly face, a wave of relief swept over him. He blurted out, "Oh Mosoom, I'm scared of my relatives. I don't think I belong here anymore."

"Wait. Don't be in such a hurry. I'm not going anyplace." Mosoom waved him over to sit down. The bear rug was soft and comfortable. "Take your time, Oskiniko, my 'young man'," he said. "Have soup with me first. We have plenty of time to talk."

They ate Mosoom's soup and bannock in an easy silence. Finally his grandfather lay back on the rug, one leg crossed over the other, his back resting against his pack. He sipped tea from a saucer like he did when Lawrence was young. His eyes rested on his grandson for a time. "Now you can tell me what you are thinking," he said.

Lawrence began, anger making his voice tremble. "I just want to live like we did before. Since I went away to school, everything has changed. I don't know what to do anymore."

Grandfather touched Lawrence gently on the shoulder. "Anger will not get you what you want. Don't feel bad. Many people I know feel the same way. Don't worry about it too much. In spite of everything, you can still speak Cree. The life you loved will come back one day. You will find a way to make it happen." Mosoom took another sip. "Come with me to the tea dance tonight. We'll start your journey back to learning the way of our people. Afterward you can stay here. We'll be home late."

After dark, Lawrence climbed up beside Mosoom on his wagon. Grandfather clicked his tongue and the horses set off at a good clip. The night air smelled sweet from the willows growing along the road.

As they passed through the countryside, Lawrence said, "I know adding and subtracting. I can read. But I feel dumber now than when I went to school."

Mosoom shook his head. "You are not dumber. Never think that again. You can read and you can count. These skills you will need as you grow older. But somehow the school just blocked your Cree thinking. You will never lose it. No matter what happens, our people will never lose what we have. Take tonight. The police won't let us have a tea dance. It's against their law. That's why we have to go out of the way to play our drums and dance."

He slowed the horses down. "Start remembering what it was like before you went to that school. Remember what I told you long ago, being good is not an easy job. It might take time to get rid of what is bothering you. You have to work at it. I don't know exactly what they do to children in that school. A lot of them never get better. You will."

They stopped in a large field. Canvas tents surrounded them. Small cooking fires glowed in the dark. Elders and children were walking from the tents to a large central fire. A group of men stood by the fire, warming their hand drums to tighten the hides and make them sound better. Families talked and laughed together, their voices raised in excitement as they waited for the singing to begin.

Soon the steady beat of the drums and Cree songs filled the air.

Lawrence felt proud. He wanted to cry when he heard the Cree singing and the drums beating. 'This is the life I love,' he thought.

People began to dance in a circle around the fire. For the first time Lawrence felt uneasy. Hearing the drums, he had a flashback of Sister Denise's voice calling him a wild savage. The drumming was like a voice that called him into the circle, but he resisted.

Suddenly Mosoom grasped his hand and led him to the circle. "Just follow me. Soon you will have all the young ladies after you."

They laughed together. The circle broke to let Grandpa and Lawrence join in. Holding Mosoom's hand and the hand of a stranger, Lawrence stepped in rhythm around the circle. With every dance, he felt more like Oskiniko again, the 'young man' so named by his grandfather long ago.

Larry Loyie in residential School

When Larry returned from residential school, he took comfort in the presence of his *Kokom* Bella Twin and *Mosoom* Edward Twin. He spent a winter on *Kokom's* trapline, learning the traditional skills of hunting, trapping and snaring. From his grandfather, he learned cultural ways and about being a good person.

Very young children were often taken from their families to live in residential schools. The schools received a small annual payment from the Canadian government for every child to pay for food, clothing and other expenses. If there was a shortage of children attending a school, students could be brought in from distant locations or were taken in as toddlers. Lawrence's best friend Isaac came from the Yukon. Because Isaac was so far from home, he did not go home for the holidays.

Lawrence loved to skate. During his school years in the mid-1940s, the boys play hockey on the rink beside the girls hall. Inside their building, the girls sat at their sewing machines and watched the boys skate.

In Aboriginal cultures, girls were taught by their mothers to sew and decorate clothing, to sew mocassins for summer and winter use, and many other skills. In this photo from St. Bernard Mission residential school, girls are taught to sew to prepare them to become wives or servants. Girls and boys were kept apart in residential schools. Even sisters and brothers were not allowed to talk to one another.

All children at residential schools did manual labour jobs. Author Larry Loyie spent six weeks of every school year picking potatoes, and four weeks stacking wood for the many furnaces at St. Bernard Mission. Other jobs were washing and polishing floors, working in the ice house and doing laundry. For girls, jobs included sewing, cooking and taking care of very young students.

Photos courtesy of La Societé Historique et Généalogique de Smoky River, Donnelly, AB.

Chapter 15 ～ Firefighting

Alphonse, the forest ranger, hurried to the log house. He knocked loudly and entered. "Kayâs," he greeted Papa. "Victor, we're in a hurry. The trucks are picking everyone up to fight the big fire in Canyon Creek. We need more men. You have experience. I need you to help me."

Papa nodded at his old friend. "I'll pack right away." In his methodical way, Papa began to gather items he needed.

Alphonse spotted Lawrence at the kitchen table. He looked him up and down, then asked, "How old are you?"

"I'll be fourteen soon."

Alphonse spoke to Papa. "Your son looks strong. This is an emergency. He has to come too."

Lawrence looked at his father. Papa said, "It will be okay. I'll watch out for you. But we have to hurry." He threw Lawrence an extra kit bag.

"What do I take?" Lawrence jumped up as he asked.

"Just face soap, a towel and a change of clothes," Papa replied.

Lawrence packed his few things in the bag. He folded a grey wool blanket for sleeping and pushed it in too.

They climbed on the back of the forestry truck and drove into town. The air was gloomy, enveloped in smoke. All over town, men were made to join the fire crew.

The truck was getting crowded. The tension in the air made Lawrence feel different. He was being treated like an experienced worker. 'Am I turning into a man overnight?' he questioned himself.

Within an hour they were on their way to Canyon Creek with a truckload of men. As they neared the fire, Lawrence saw a policeman pull a car over. The man sitting beside Lawrence leaned toward him and said, "If you're not working, you have two choices. You can firefight or you can go to jail. That's what the police are telling them."

When it was their turn to pass, the policeman waved them on.

At the camp, a foreman told all the young people to stand aside. Lawrence stood with a group of boys.

Most of them looked older than him.

The foreman spoke seriously. "None of you have ever fought a fire before. Let me tell you, it's not fun. It's a dangerous job and I want you all to be careful. Don't think you can fool the fire. It's bigger than any of you are."

He wiped his forehead with a smudged handkerchief. "A few years ago there was a fire in the small town of Assineau. That fire burned everything up. People got trapped behind it. They had to lie down in the creek to survive. If you get caught, remember this. If there's any water around, head for it and stay there."

The foreman placed the men in groups of eight. Lawrence found himself with his cousin Leo. At eighteen years of age, Leo was already a man.

"We have to get our Wajax," Leo explained. "That's a pack filled with water. You pump the water out at the fire." He handed Lawrence a shovel and picked up an axe for himself.

The foreman sent two older men to check a small burn nearby. Then he pointed to Leo and Lawrence. "You two go farther up and see if there's any more fires like that one. When you're done, come back here."

Carrying their equipment, they set out. At first the fire was at a distance. Lawrence watched it with awe as it popped and burned ahead of them. Suddenly, he felt the wind shift and saw the hill behind them catch fire. The flames moved closer, as if pushed by an unseen hand.

"We're cut off," Lawrence yelled at Leo.

Over the sound of roaring flames, Leo screamed back. "We've got to run. Come on. Bring your shovel and Wajax! We must keep the water."

They started running. The fire kept up, filling in behind them. Their equipment was heavy and slowed them down. 'I don't even know where we are,' Lawrence thought with horror.

Thick smoke filled the air. Lawrence could barely breathe. He was soaked with sweat. He followed Leo. His cousin finally stopped, his eyes wide with fear, staring out from a face blackened by ashes. Saying nothing, the two pushed on, darting across burning piles of brush.

Lawrence tripped, then picked himself back up. 'I'm not going to die in this fire,' he swore. "You're not going to get me," he shouted in anger.

In the distance, he heard men hollering their names.

"We're here, we're in the fire," the boys yelled. Lawrence's voice cracked from the smoke, but he yelled again and again.

At last they heard a man calling back. It was the foreman's voice and he seemed closer now. "Come straight for our voices," the foreman shouted. "We can hear you. We'll keep hollering for you!"

Almost collapsing, they burst out of the smoke-filled forest into a clearing. The main camp was only a few hundred metres ahead of them.

Lawrence began to shake. He finally felt fear, real fear, when he saw the firefighters safely ahead. He had a terrifying thought. 'I could have died back there. Leo and I could have burned to death. If I died today, where would I spend eternity?'

He tried not to look afraid, but it was hard to hide.

The foreman ran toward them. "Thank God you guys made it," he said. Relief filled his voice. "We thought you were goners for sure. The fire moved so fast you got cut off from the main group. You really earned your pay today."

Lawrence had never heard sweeter words.

~

The next morning, bacon was frying in a skillet and boiled eggs bubbled on a hot cauldron. The firefighters in the camp ate until they were stuffed.

Lawrence recognized Muxseem, the bone game player, going for his breakfast. The huge man was walking barefoot to the fire. "He thinks more of his bacon than he does of his feet," Lawrence said to Leo. They watched Muxseem pick his way daintily across the clearing, his big belly swaying.

As he neared the fire pit, a piece of burning charcoal sparked upward and landed right between Muxseem's toes. Jumping and hopping around on one foot, Muxseem bobbed and screeched. "Yow! Help me!" he shouted.

"What's wrong with him?" Leo asked.

"I don't know. I can't see," Lawrence said.

"My toes! It's my toes! They're burning," Muxseem yelled frantically. A man with a cup of hot tea rushed forward. He splashed the liquid on Muxseem's foot. The big man collapsed on a stump. "That feels better," he moaned. He didn't seem to feel the heat of the tea that had put out the hot coal.

After that, the foreman told Muxseem to stay in camp and help the cook.

"He'll be happy now," Lawrence told Leo. "He can eat all he wants in the cook tent."

Chapter 16 ~ Flying

Lawrence looked at his statement from Forestry. After seventeen days of firefighting, he had made one hundred and fifteen dollars. For Lawrence, it was a fortune. Papa told him, "You can take your statement to Vance's general store and buy whatever you want now. When your cheque comes, it will go to the store. You'll get whatever is left over."

At the general store, Lawrence bought a second pair of Cowboy King jeans. Now he had a pair for going out. The storekeeper gave him a cash advance of twenty dollars as well. Lawrence liked the feeling of independence. He could buy anything he wanted.

Walking downtown, he saw a Cree boy standing in front of the pool hall. He recognized Johnny Jackson. No one ever called him Johnny when they spoke of him. They always said his full name: Johnny Jackson. His brothers were good baseball players and Johnny played too. He was small for a ball player but what he lacked in size he made up in ability.

"Hi, Johnny," Lawrence said.

Johnny grinned at him. "Come and shoot a game of pool, Lawrence. I need somebody to play with."

"I want to, but I don't know how to play pool. Besides, I can't go in. I'm not old enough and my dad's not around."

"Don't worry about it." Johnny smiled coolly. "Jo-Jo's in charge today and he won't say anything. He knows my dad. My dad will be your dad today in the pool hall." He opened the door and they both walked into the dim interior of the poolroom.

Johnny pulled a pool cue from a rack and laid it over the table. "Here's how you do it." He showed Lawrence. "Put your hand flat and put your cue on it. Put the cue between your pointer finger and thumb. Rest the cue there. It's the steadiest bridge you can have."

Lawrence bent over the table and carefully sized up his shot. He hit a ball with a whack. It bounced once and flew into the pocket.

Johnny's eyes crinkled with laughter. "Did you say this was your first game? Am I playing with a pool shark here?"

Shook up, Lawrence missed his next shot.

"Now it's my turn," Johnny said. He smoothly

pocketed a cue ball. "What have you been doing lately?"

"I went firefighting in Canyon Creek. I just about didn't make it back."

"I heard that," Johnny said. "I was there too. Not where you were, though. I would have seen you." He narrowly missed the next pocket.

It was Lawrence's turn again. He missed, but came closer than before. He eased up and asked, "What are you doing now?"

"Playing baseball." Johnny shot the last ball into the pocket. "That's it, I win." He stored the cue on the rack. "Why don't we go outside and play catch for a while. We have time before I go home for supper."

They went out to the lot in front of the poolroom. Johnny handed Lawrence his practice glove and showed him how to put it on. He wore his playing glove and threw Lawrence an easy catch.

"This is the first time I ever played catch with a glove," Lawrence told him.

"You're doing great," Johnny said. He threw the next catch harder and Lawrence caught it easily. They played until it was time for supper.

Other than his cousins, this was the first time Lawrence had made a friend outside of the Mission school. Johnny Jackson was a great guy. Lawrence walked happily home, looking forward to the day he could play catch again with the best ball player in town.

~

His father was waiting for him at the log house. "There's a job for you in Little Whitefish Lake. I signed you on. I'm going that way by pack horses through the bush. You'll be flying in. Go see the foreman to confirm. The pay is ten dollars clear a day for thirty days."

The job was working for an American oil company, a seismograph team from Texas doing surveying. The next morning, with his bedroll and a change of clothes, Lawrence met a truck that took him to the Lesser Slave Lake dock at Faust where workers were busy loading equipment onto a twin engine float plane.

"Did you ever fly before?" a man asked Lawrence in Cree.

"When would I get a chance to fly?" Lawrence shot back. He stared warily at the plane. It looked small for all the men and cargo.

"Guess we're all new at it," said another man.

"What do you have to do when you fly?" Lawrence asked a man he knew. His name was Dave, and like Papa, he had been in the First and Second World Wars.

Dave looked thoughtful. "Make sure you go to the toilet as often as you can before you get on the plane."

"There's no toilet on the plane?"

"No, kid. And you don't want to have to do a number two up there."

Lawrence couldn't tell for sure, but it seemed like Dave was laughing at him. Dave tapped the bedroll under Lawrence's arm. "I see you got your bedroll. What's them things in it? Books?"

"Cowboy books." Lawrence tucked them carefully inside his blanket.

They boarded the plane. The workers sat on webbed seats on both sides. The pilot put the plane in motion and taxied farther out on the lake. Once in place, the pilot said, "We're taking off now. Hang onto your seats." The engines roared and the plane skimmed over the water, bouncing on the waves like on a washboard. Suddenly, they were in the air, flying over bush country. The engines sputtered as the plane levelled out. Lawrence's stomach dropped. Were they going down? He looked out the window. They were still in the air. That was good. He looked around. Sure enough, there was no place to go to the toilet.

Lawrence looked out again. From above, the trees were tiny. Specks of boats dotted Lesser Slave Lake. All too soon for Lawrence, they were landing in Little Whitefish Lake.

The huge American-run camp was surrounded by forest. The kitchen tent was so big that when it rained the entire crew could eat inside. Bigger sleeping tents stood nearby, filled with cots. Lawrence chose a cot by the door and put his kit bag on top of it.

The boss was a Texan named Omar. He was a tall, good-looking man who had an easy way of handling the crew. "You'll be a swamper and help the power saw man," he told Lawrence. "Fred from Canyon Creek is the power saw man." Lawrence nodded but had a hard time understanding Omar's Texan accent.

The next day, Lawrence and Fred started out early to walk into the bush. Fred carried the power saw. Lawrence carried a can of gas needed for the power saw.

The axe men had gone ahead using poles to make

sure the line was straight for one mile. Fred and Lawrence came behind them to cut a road wide enough for a machine to go through.

Before he started the power saw, Fred told Lawrence to stand back. He warned him, "There's no clutch for the chain. The saw won't stop unless I shut the motor off. If you fall on it and it's still going, it will rip you to shreds."

The power saw roared, chewing at the thick willow bushes. Lawrence stepped far back whenever Fred used it.

He was relieved when Omar assigned him to another job. "The power saw job is too heavy for you, kid," Omar said. "I want you to help in the cook tent instead."

One day, Papa arrived with a pack train of nineteen horses and eight saddle horses. As he unpacked the non-perishable camp food and other supplies, Lawrence stood by and talked to him. It was good to see his father again.

"How is it going, son?" Papa asked as he hauled down a box of canned fruit.

"I like it here. I like being in the bush."

"I thought you would. You don't have any rules here. Just do your job and do it well."

The next morning, when everyone was gone from camp into the bush, Lawrence visited with Simon Cardinal. The easy-going Cree horse wrangler was packing three horses to bring food to another camp down the line.

"Do you want to learn how to tie the diamond hitch?" Simon asked. The complicated diamond hitch was used to tie the packs on the horses. Step by step, Simon showed Lawrence how to tie it. By the third horse, Lawrence knew the diamond hitch inside and out.

"You're a fast learner." Simon whistled. "Not many people know how to do the diamond hitch."

The thirty days in camp passed quickly. Along with his three hundred dollars in pay, Lawrence took home the knowledge of how to tie the diamond hitch.

Chapter 17 ~ Harvest Time

Uncle Moses and Lawrence were sitting outside reading when his uncle asked, "Do you want to go harvesting with me?"

"No," Lawrence said sullenly.

"Don't you want to work?"

"I went to a farm with my brother Robert and my cousin Leo to pick rocks and roots. They left and never came back. I had to hitchhike home. I only had a peanut butter sandwich. It took two days to get home."

"That won't happen this time," Uncle Moses said. "We're going to Pibroch. It's a granary stop on the railway line. A farmer hires as many men as he needs to harvest five or six farms. If you want to work, Pibroch is where to go."

"It sounds good. I'll go."

Lawrence liked his uncle. He had once taken Lawrence with him to his trapline to show him life in the bush. Uncle Moses always had books in his cabin, hidden away where the mice couldn't get them.

The day they arrived in Pibroch, Farmer Raines was doing the hiring. Right away, he hired Lawrence and Roy, a Cree man from Wabasca. "You two will start with stooking," Raines told them. "I'm paying ten dollars a day."

"Aren't you coming with us?" Lawrence asked Uncle Moses with a worried look.

"I'll be nearby at a farm I worked on last summer. If it rains, come into Westlock. We can meet in the poolroom," Uncle Moses said.

The farm was located down a gravel road. It was a well-kept spread with milking cows and horses. A tractor was parked in the yard ready for use. Lawrence and Roy shared a room in the shed. Roy was tall and well built for a middle-aged man but he already had a paunch and he liked his smoke breaks. In a few days, Roy was sent to work at another farm.

Raines asked Lawrence to stay on. That evening, lying on his bed, Lawrence wondered why the farmer had chosen for him to stay. 'He chose me over an experienced man,' he thought. 'I'll show him he made a good choice. I'll earn my ten dollars a day.'

The workday started at sunrise. The bundling

machine dropped eight bundles of cut grain on every drop, all in rows. The farmer showed Lawrence how to stack the eight heavy bundles together into a tidy stook by standing them up against each other. Once the bundles dried, a wagon with a hayrack on it came along to pick them up. Every day, Raines and Lawrence worked until sunset.

He ate all his meals with the family. The Raines had four children, two girls and two boys. Mrs. Raines's table was always piled high with meat, vegetables and fresh-baked buns.

The youngest in the family was Mark. He was chubby and friendly. The two girls, Ethel and Darlene, were cheery teenagers who liked to talk. Ethel had huge blue eyes, while Darlene's were green. They both had straight light–brown hair, held back with clips. Tony, the older boy, was skinny even though he ate a lot. His hair was slicked back and he hardly ever smiled.

"Where are you from, Lawrence?" Darlene asked one night.

"From Slave Lake northwest of here."

"She knows where Slave Lake is," Tony interrupted.

"Is this your first job?" Ethel asked.

"I was firefighting before. Then I worked in Little

Whitefish Lake for an American oil camp. I flew in."
The girls' eyes widened.

"Are you through with school already?" Tony butt
in again. "You couldn't have finished grade eight. I'm
working on my grade ten."

Mr. Raines looked up from his plate. "He's a hard
worker, that's why he's here," he said in his gruff
voice, then continued eating.

Mrs. Raines spoke quietly to Lawrence. "Now that
Fred is gone, you can move into the house. There's a
cot in the playroom. You can sleep on that. You are
one of the family now." She stood up and began to
clear away the dishes.

Lawrence watched her move about the kitchen
in her motherly way. Then he stepped outside. The
evening air was cool after an afternoon shower. He
spotted Mark standing near the tractor and walked
over.

"Let's go play in the hayloft. Ethel and Darlene
are already there," Mark said.

They started walking to the barn.

"How old are you?" Mark asked.

"Just about fourteen. I'll be fifteen next year."

"I'm twelve. Tony and Darlene are not my real
family. They're my adopted cousins. They don't

have parents anymore."

A hazy light glowed inside the barn. The two girls stood side by side high above them on one of the rafters. "Watch me," Ethel shouted. She grabbed a rope and swung out over the deep hay. Then she let go. Darlene swung next.

"C'mon Lawrence, it's your turn," Ethel shouted.

Soon Lawrence and Mark were swinging with them. As he played with the children, Lawrence forgot all about hard work.

~

The next day, Farmer Raines explained the set-up for threshing. "We'll thresh six farms with ten teams of horses all within a four-mile radius. We'll start from the furthest and work in. Mark will show you how to get to the first farm." Lawrence and Mark drove the wagon with a hayrack attached. Ten teams of men and horses met them at the first of the farms. They ate every day where they worked. When one farm was finished, they moved on to the next. Lawrence's job was to lift the bundles of grain with a pitchfork. He was filling out and getting stronger every day.

One day, Raines piled the three boys with him into his car to drive to Westlock. He stopped in front of the farm store. He stepped out and Tony joined him on the sidewalk.

Lawrence and Mark stood beside the car. Raines nodded to them. "You two come back here in an hour. Have an ice cream or something."

The streets of Westlock were dusty. Mark and Lawrence walked along one side of town, planning to walk back up the other side.

"Tony said he heard that a Zoot Suiter gang was coming to Westlock to clean up the town," Mark said. "Then they'll take it over."

"What's a Zoot Suiter?" Lawrence had never heard of the gang before.

"They're a bunch of tough guys who wear funny clothes. They always wear purple and black. Their pants are baggy and tight around the ankles. They wear lots of chains hanging down from their belts."

"Kind of like a comic book character," Lawrence laughed. Looking down the nearly empty streets of Westlock, he didn't see much to clean up.

They strolled along, passing a couple of stores and a garage. Up ahead, a group of four boys walked toward them. They were teenagers, older than

Lawrence and Mark. They jostled one another as they got closer. They were shouting but Lawrence couldn't make out what they were saying.

"Do you know those guys?" Lawrence asked Mark.

Before Mark could answer, the town boys stopped in front of them. They stared at Lawrence, saying nothing. The tallest boy stepped forward. "Hey, there's an Indian kid," he said.

"I never seen him here before," said the burly teenager beside him.

"He could be one of them Zoot Suiters," a skinny boy said.

"We better teach him a lesson," said a boy with messy hair.

The town boys began to move toward them. Lawrence stood there, not knowing what to do. He'd never met up with bullies before. Anger clutched his chest in a tight band. 'Sister Denise, you won't hit me again,' his mind screamed. He clenched his fists and raised them high. The town boys looked tough, but he was sure he could heave one or two of them like a grain bundle.

Mark stood beside him. "He's not a Zoot Suiter. He works for my dad," he yelled. The town boys stepped back.

Suddenly Farmer Raines appeared. He towered over the town boys. "You leave the kid alone," he growled.

"We weren't doing nothing," the burly boy said.

"You just leave him alone. Now get out of here."

The boys scattered. The farmer turned to Lawrence and Mark. "You did well, boys. You just needed a little backup," he said with a grin. "Let's get going. We have to be home by supper." Walking beside Lawrence, Mark smiled. Lawrence smiled back at him. He and his white friend had done well together.

The log house was empty when Lawrence returned home. A month ago it was filled with his brothers and sisters. While he was on the farm, the truck had come to take the younger ones back to school. Papa was away on a pack trip and Elizabeth was working as a waitress in a café in Edmonton for the Canadian National Railway.

"I didn't even get to say goodbye," Lawrence said out loud. For the first time in his life he was alone with no routine to follow, free to do what he wanted. He went farther up Rabbit Hill to visit Kokom. As usual, she greeted him with a hug. He was at least a head taller than her now. He realized that he had grown over the summer.

Kokom put more water in her teakettle and set it on the cook stove. She turned to him and said in Cree, "My, how you have grown. Sit. I want to hear what you have been doing. Uncle Moses told me you went farming with him."

"I had to work hard to keep up with the men but I did it," Lawrence said proudly. "I had blisters on my hands. One of the guys told me to pee on them and it would make them tougher. I just couldn't do it. Sometimes I wanted to; they hurt so much. After a while my hands got tough, too."

Kokom laughed. "You always learned fast. Remember when you used to stay with us at old Camp Six? That sawmill was a ten-mile walk out in the woods. It was nothing for you, even though you were little."

"I remember when your dog, Maskwa, was killed by a cougar. You were so angry at that killer."

Grandma frowned at the memory of losing one of her best friends. "I certainly was. It was good in them days to have my grandchildren with me."

She poured him a cup of tea and passed him some bannock with homemade jam. "Your mama made the best blueberry jam. She took you to the sand ridges by the lake many times to show you the berries and medicine plants. You were only three and four years old. Do you remember those days?"

Lawrence nodded. "I used to carry the tobacco for Mama. She put it down to thank the plants. She told me she was putting something back for what she took out."

Searching his memory, he could see himself and his mother walking along the sand ridges. The sun was rising. His mother bent down to pick a leaf and held it up to show him.

"I remember the medicines were still green. The berries weren't ripe yet."

Kokom poured more tea. "Some of the medicines are less bitter when they're young. Later in the year they get really bitter though they are still as good."

They sat quietly. Then Kokom sighed. "Your mother knew our medicines from the old days. She was like her father, your Mosoom Edward. Never forget the lessons she taught you."

Lawrence rose to go. As he headed down the hill, Kokom called after him. "I'd like you to come with me to my trapline this winter. Uncle Moses will be there. We'd like to have you with us."

"I will come with you, Kokom," Lawrence decided quickly. Her invitation made him feel like one of the family again. As he walked back to the empty house, Lawrence looked forward to his winter on the trapline.

~

The morning after Papa returned, he made fresh coffee and toasted hot bannock with jam and butter for the two of them. "I talked to your Uncle Louis and asked if he would go hunting moose with me," Papa told Lawrence. "He said he would be here this morning."

"I'm going hunting with you and Uncle Louis," Lawrence said.

When Uncle Louis arrived, Lawrence followed him quietly, watching his every move. When the three of them were well into the forest, his uncle stopped and pointed to some tracks. "A moose was here less than an hour ago. We must be extra quiet. Moose can hear much better than we do."

They moved carefully. Suddenly, Uncle Louis tapped Lawrence's arm. He pointed ahead to where two moose stood feeding. His uncle raised his gun. In a swift movement, Lawrence started to raise his gun as well. Uncle Louis shook his head.

"Peyak poko," he whispered. "One only." With a skilled shot, Uncle Louis brought down the larger of the two moose. The second moose vanished into the forest.

Before they prepared the moose, they had to let

it lie a couple of hours. "The moose meat will be softer that way," Uncle Louis explained. "Your dad will go and get Kokom. She will help us cut and dry the meat."

While they waited, Uncle Louis built a fire, made tea and gave his nephew a piece of bannock to eat with it. "I know you wanted to shoot your first moose," he said to Lawrence. "These days, moose are scarce. Now we know there's another one in the area when we need food again."

By late afternoon, Papa returned with Kokom. They began to cut the meat into strips for drying and smoking.

His uncle cut a piece of the moose's heart and put it in the fire. "I'm thanking the moose for giving its life to feed us," he said.

For the next few days, they stayed in the bush, drying and smoking the meat over the fire. Then they put the meat in gunny sacks ready for transportation. With satisfied looks they surveyed the neatly tied bundles. "Everything is ready to go now," Kokom said.

As Uncle Louis gathered his few belongings, Papa added, "Send a taxi to pick us up. We'll stay the night here. We'll be waiting at the road in the morning."

In the Mission school, Lawrence had lain awake after the lights were out, remembering the good times with his family. Every summer, they had travelled by horse and wagon to their camp by the river. Night after night, he had dreamed of that way of life. Now, watching Uncle Louis leave, he realized the days of horses and wagons were over. As they waited for the taxi, Lawrence was grateful that he could spend one more winter with Kokom on her trapline.

CHAPTER 19 ~ HEADING WEST

Lawrence looked out the window of the Northern Alberta Railway coach and saw nothing but darkness. He had boarded the train at midnight so he could be in Edmonton early in the morning. He stared at the letter in his hand from his sister Elizabeth. "Come with me to McBride, British Columbia, near the Rocky Mountains," she wrote. "I have a job waiting at the Beanery Café of the Canadian National Railway. My boss is sending me there."

Lawrence was a little afraid. British Columbia was something new. With Papa away with the pack train, he went to Kokom's to say he was leaving. "I won't be coming with you again to the trapline this winter," he told her. "I'm going with Elizabeth to see the Rocky Mountains." His voice quivered with excitement, but there was also sadness at leaving her. "I learned a lot last winter with you on the trapline. I will never forget those days."

"I'm happy for you, Grandson," Kokom said simply. "I was born in those same mountains. I often think of them. You might not want to come back. There's something about those mountains that make you want to stay." With tears in her eyes, Kokom kissed him goodbye.

The train click-clacked its way to the city. He looked again at the address on the envelope: Mr. Lawrence Loyie, General Delivery, Slave Lake, Alberta. 'What is my new address going to be? What lies ahead for me?' he wondered.

As the train neared Edmonton, he took courage. 'I've been stuck before and had to hitchhike home. Now I have money of my own. I can take a bus or a train anytime I want. I saved up for an adventure. I'm glad it's going to be with my sister,' he thought.

Elizabeth met him at the train station. They spent the day exploring Edmonton. In Eaton's department store, Lawrence bought himself a pair of shiny black and brown CCM skates. They had a nice, light feel to them and he was proud to carry them out of the store. Elizabeth took him to eat at a Chinese café. He'd never tried that kind of food before. He was leery at first about trying new foods in a public place, but his sister reassured him it was good. And it was.

The next morning, Lawrence bought his ticket to McBride and they boarded the day coach. As they pulled out of Edmonton on the 6:30 a.m. train, he was glad they were on their way. He didn't care for the city with its crowds and bad smells.

The conductor came by and punched their tickets. Farm after farm passed as they relaxed in the plush train seats and talked for hours like they did back home.

"Do you remember the stories we used to tell late at night?" Elizabeth asked.

"Remember The Three Robin Hood Kids?" Lawrence chuckled. "You made it up. Those kids were always trying to make things right in the world."

"Yeah! That was you, Margaret and me," Elizabeth said.

"Remember when we went with Papa to pick raspberries? We got chased by the cows. The little ones ran around screaming their heads off."

"Papa was angry but he just went on picking berries." Elizabeth smiled. "He would send you to get fresh cream to eat with our berries."

As the train pulled into Edson to take on water they sat quietly, remembering the good times. A few minutes later they crossed a high wooden trestle over an eddy of the McLeod River. The river in the valley far below glistened in the sun.

"Hinton. Last stop before Jasper," the conductor called as he walked along the swaying aisle.

"There's something I've never told you before." Lawrence paused, unsure about revealing his secret. "When I was in the hospital in High Prairie, I read a fancy magazine. It had a story by a guy named Ernest Hemingway. Ever since then I've dreamed about being a writer."

Elizabeth was not surprised at all. She only said, "You enjoy all kinds of books. Not like me. I'm stuck on romance stories and movie magazines."

Past Hinton, the mighty Athabasca River spread out more like a lake than a river. Lawrence stared out the window watching the mountains get closer by the minute. All he had seen before were pictures of mountains that didn't impress him much. They looked no bigger than little Marten Mountain back home. But soon the Rockies towered in the distance, their snowy peaks jutting against the sky. The sight of them made Lawrence's heart beat faster. The giant slabs of granite were powerful and haunting and the most beautiful scenery he had ever seen. Soon they seemed within touching distance. He peered straight up beside the side of the railway tracks. On a craggy ledge above him, he saw a white mountain goat standing alone.

"Thank you, Sister Theresa," he whispered to the distant peaks.

At Jasper, Lawrence and Elizabeth changed trains for the five-hour trip to McBride. As the train left the resort town, Elizabeth frowned at Lawrence. "Are you all right?" she asked. "You haven't said anything for a while."

"I was thinking about the Camp Four sawmill," Lawrence replied. "I worked there after I spent last winter with Kokom. The men put in six days a week and partied on the seventh. The parties were fun at first but they always got too noisy. It was always the same, week after week. After a while, I said I was too young to go along. There were lots of books for me to read in the bunkhouse."

They passed Tête Jaune, one of the last stops before McBride. On their left, the Fraser River widened. The Rocky Mountains hovered beyond the river across a level valley. 'This is the life I want,' Lawrence thought. 'There's more to life than working all week and partying all weekend.'

"One thing I did like about Camp Four," he told his sister. "Everybody there spoke Cree. I learned more, talking to them."

As they neared McBride, the Fraser River curled beside the train track. Lawrence felt rising excitement as they pulled into the station platform.

McBride was a small village in the Robson Valley. It seemed as if the whole town was out on the platform waiting for the train. Some boarded the train to leave for Prince George and points beyond. The Rocky Mountains to the north and the Cariboo Mountains to the south pushed in toward the village. McBride Peak on Mount Teare seemed so close Lawrence fancied he could climb it in an hour.

"I love McBride," he said to Elizabeth. "I could stay here forever."

"That's the café where I'll be working." She pointed inside the station. The Beanery Café had a big window that looked out onto the platform. Elizabeth was pleased. "I'll be the first to see who gets off the train. Who knows? Maybe some famous movie star will get off one day."

His sister strode out of the station carrying her suitcase. Lawrence hurried to keep up. "We're staying with cousin Adele and her husband, Frank. They live across the river," Elizabeth said. She walked to a taxi nearby, got in, and told the driver their destination.

Chapter 20 ~ The Green Chain

Lawrence and James walked along the gravel highway. James whistled as he walked. He was from Saskatchewan and almost twice as old as Lawrence.

"I'm going back to work at the sawmill tonight," James said happily. "Come downtown with me. We might run into the foreman who hired me. Maybe he has a job for you."

Walking along Main Street, a man was coming toward them. "That's the foreman," James said. "He might need more men. Cree men are good workers."

The foreman was tall and red-faced. He stopped when he got to James and Lawrence.

"I got another guy for you," James said.

The foreman looked Lawrence up and down. "He's kind of small, isn't he?"

Lawrence wanted to smack the foreman in the mouth. He didn't need anyone to say he was small.

He could do a man's work any day. He imagined the foreman backhanding him with one of his beefy hands. Lawrence pictured taking him on, like the bodybuilder, Charles Atlas, and not like some ninety-seven pound weakling in the comic books.

James spoke breezily. "Good things come in small packages."

"That's true." The foreman turned to Lawrence. "What did you do before?"

"I worked at Camp Four sawmill. Before that, I harvested from dawn to dusk." Lawrence stood taller, pushing his chest out. "I worked as hard as any man in that outfit. The farmer who hired me got his money's worth."

"Try him," James said encouragingly.

The foreman moved on. Over his shoulder, he spoke, "Be there with James. You can start tonight."

James grinned. "You're on, Lawrence, night shift. We start at eight and finish at six in the morning, half an hour for lunch."

At seven that night, they walked into town to catch their ride to the mill. The driver was a friend of James. They carried moose steak sandwiches and thermoses of coffee for their lunch. The mill was out of town along a well-kept gravel road. The snow was piled high on both sides. Trucks hauled lumber from the mill to the lumberyard.

As they drove to the sawmill, James said, "You'll be starting on the green chain. I'll be canting. We get ten cents more an hour to work the night shift."

The mill appeared before them, lit brightly by the yellow glow of spotlights. Inside, Lawrence signed the time sheet and did the necessary paperwork. Then the foreman took him outside to the green chain. The bitterly cold night air slammed into Lawrence as he stepped into the open yard of the mill.

"This is Harold. You'll be working with him," the foreman said.

Harold was a grizzled older man with a red face half-hidden under a thick hat with long earflaps. He was bundled in layers of clothes that made him waddle when he walked. "Can he handle it?" Harold challenged the foreman.

"You just do your job," the foreman ordered him.

The whistle blew and work began. Lumber soon slid down the green chain. Lawrence hauled off his first piece. It was two-by-eight, sixteen feet long, frozen and slippery. It was heavy but he knew it would be. 'I'll show that guy,' he promised himself.

In no time, Lawrence was hustling back and forth pulling lumber off the green chain. He piled them according to sizes and lengths. When a pile was high enough, a truck backed in and hauled the lumber away.

It didn't take him long to learn that Harold did half as much work. Lawrence had to push himself to keep up with the boards sliding down the green chain. He glared at Harold but the man didn't move any faster. The harder Lawrence worked, the warmer he got. 'At least I won't freeze to death,' he thought grimly.

Stars still glinted in the dark sky when the shift was over. "That was a piece of cake," he mumbled to James. He fell asleep on the short ride back to town.

~

"Wake up, Leonard." Lawrence shook his young cousin, Adele's son, in the seat next to him.

"Hunh? What's happening?" Leonard opened his eyes and looked around. The last of the audience was leaving the McBride movie house.

"Darn it. We fell asleep and missed the movie." Lawrence stomped up the aisle. Leonard ran after him to keep up. "I was looking forward to that musical," Lawrence grumbled. "I've never fallen asleep in a movie before."

He knew why it had happened and it only made him angrier. It was Harold, lazy Harold, back at the sawmill.

'That's it,' he told himself. 'Three weeks is enough. I'm not going to do his work anymore. I'll talk to the foreman on Monday. I'll tell him I'm going to quit if Harold doesn't do his job.' The more Lawrence thought about it, the angrier he got. 'I'll whack Harold in the head with a two-by-four. That'll wake him up.'

The foreman was surprised to see Lawrence before the night shift whistle blew. "Is something wrong?" he asked.

The words tumbled out of Lawrence's mouth before he could stop them. "I'm leaving. I'm going to walk off the job unless there's a change. That Harold makes me do all the work."

"If you can't do your job...," the foreman started to say.

Lawrence cut him off. "I can do my job." He heard the anger throbbing in his own voice and it frightened him. The foreman's face loomed before him, his eyes wary.

Lawrence forced himself to take a deep breath. Getting angry only made him feel bad and hurting others made it worse. He wasn't going to back down, that was true. But he knew he didn't need to blow up either. The foreman was listening to him now.

He tried to smile. "I can do my job. I am doing my job and half of his. If Harold won't do his share of work, get someone to work with me who can."

The foreman nodded. "Take it easy. I've been watching you. I know you're doing more than your share of work. I'll set it right."

"I hope you do," Lawrence said.

The foreman walked off. As Lawrence watched him head for the green chain, he felt better. He didn't have to fight to get what he wanted, just stand up for himself. He could be assertive without having to get angry. It was a good feeling.

Chapter 21 ~ Skating

For Lawrence, skating was a natural pastime. He always had an audience when he was on the ice. When school was out, his cousin Leonard and Leonard's friend John would head across the Fraser River to watch him. They stood in their skates by the edge of the back eddy, staring as he swept around the willow bushes that dotted the ice. Lawrence made an extra circle as fast as he could, then skated up to them and stopped with a scraping of ice. The two boys stood with their mouths open.

"How do you do that?" Leonard asked. He was a skinny little guy with skates too big for him. "You're the greatest skater I ever seen."

"Will you teach us how to skate forward and backward?" John asked. He was almost Lawrence's age and still in school.

"Don't you know how to skate?"

"Sure, but not fancy."

Lawrence thought of the many nights cleaning

the rink overlooking Buffalo Bay. He'd skated hard on that little rink. Here the ice reached out in all directions. He could really get up some speed.

"Okay, I'll teach you but it takes a lot of practice to do turns."

He spent the afternoons showing them his tricks. He could skate backward, make circles, turn left and right and skate fast. His shiny new CCM skates flashed across the ice. 'CCMs, the skates of champions,' he thought.

Two girls showed up. They were both about fifteen years old. One was a Cree. Her dark hair was brushed around her face in a Tony perm. Curls peeped out from under her wool hat. Her eyes twinkled with mischief. The other was a white girl. Her curly light–brown hair hung loosely on her shoulders. Neither girl wore skates.

The Cree girl stepped boldly forward on the ice. "John told me about you. He said you were a really good skater. We came down to see you skate."

John pushed between the two girls. "Her name's Lena. She's my sister," he crowed.

Lawrence skated away from them. He picked up speed and turned with a quick flip. He was going backward now and could watch the shapes in their dark winter coats at the edge of the ice. He flipped around and scooted down the ice toward them.

"That was so good," Lena laughed with excitement. Her eyes shone when she looked at him.

Lawrence smiled back. "It's easy when you practise as long as I have."

The white girl spoke for the first time. "Will you teach me how to skate like that?"

"Do you have skates?"

"They're at home. I'll bring them next time. I'm not very good at skating," she admitted.

"What's your name?" Lawrence asked her. He liked her voice. It was friendly and sounded like she was happy.

"Thelma."

"I can teach you both, if you want me to."

Lena shrugged her shoulders. She wasn't smiling at him now. "If I have time," she sniffed. "I might be busy."

"Will you be here Saturday?" Thelma asked.

"Sure, I'll be here. I don't work on Saturday."

"See you Saturday, then." Thelma shivered. "I better go home. It's getting cold out here."

"I've got to go too," Lena said. The two friends left together.

John made kissing noises. "I think Lena's got eyes for Lawrence. And so has Thelma."

"Don't tease me or you won't get any skating lessons," Lawrence warned. He skated off to hide his big smile.

~

As he walked along the path, Lawrence wondered if Thelma was going to show up. He didn't have a clear view of the skating area. Tall willow bushes grew in clumps out of the frozen back eddies. Before freeze up, water had overflowed from the river. Now the ice was glassy smooth and barely covered with snow.

Rounding a bush he saw her sitting on a log. 'She's very pretty,' he thought.

He put his skates down on the ice. "I'll tie your skates," he offered. He knelt in front of her. She was wearing a blue cap that made her eyes look bright blue.

Thelma looked back then dropped her eyes. "You can tie them tighter," she said with a giggle. He laughed too and pulled harder on the laces. "That's good. I can never get them tight enough," she said.

Thelma stood up. Her arms shot up. She almost fell and grabbed him to keep steady.

Lawrence held her a moment. "Sit down while I put on my skates."

He slipped into his skates. Hand in hand they skated around the back eddies.

"I'll pull you," he said and began picking up speed.

"Not so fast! We're going to fall down!" Thelma protested. Once she almost tripped but caught herself. Their laughter echoed along the river.

The back eddies were fun to skate around. The sun was shining and the wind wasn't strong. Thelma's cheeks turned pink.

"Let's have a rest," Lawrence suggested. They found a log to sit on. Thelma pulled her coat down around her.

Adjusting her wool cap snugly around her ears, she asked, "You don't go to school, do you?"

Her question made him angry but he wasn't sure why. His face flushed and she looked at him curiously.

"I'm finished with school," he finally said. He didn't want to talk about the Mission, but he found himself telling her about it. "I hated the school I went to. I never wanted to go back there again."

Thelma nodded and Lawrence found her easy to talk to. He felt more relaxed now. "What grade are you in?" he asked.

"I'm in grade ten. We're learning algebra and geometry."

"I always wanted to learn algebra and geometry. I know they're math."

"They're kind of hard." She made a face.

"I learned to do something hard. It's called the diamond hitch."

"What's a diamond hitch?"

"It's a special hitch that's used for packing horses. Not many people know how to do it because it's complicated. You show me how to do algebra and geometry and I'll show you how to tie a diamond hitch."

"I would like that very much." She laughed. "I really mean it." She stood up and brushed the snow off her coat. "We'd better skate some more before we get too cold."

Far off, Lawrence could see Leonard and John practising their skating turns. His eyes drifted along the ice. Something seemed to be moving behind a bush. He didn't have time to look again. Without warning, Thelma fell down, catching Lawrence by surprise. He helped her up, his arm around her waist. Her eyes met his again. Her eyes were so beautiful. He moved closer and kissed her. Neither said anything as they started off again.

He saw movement again in a clump of bushes but said nothing to Thelma.

The next time Thelma fell, it was backward into a snowdrift. Lawrence felt a tug from her hand as she went down and he fell on top of her. Their lips were close already so he kissed her again, this time with more feeling.

They looked at each other for a moment. Then Lawrence frowned. Once again he noticed a far-off shadow or movement. He rolled onto the snowdrift.

"What's the matter?" Thelma asked.

"I saw something. I'm sure someone is spying on us." They both looked around but nothing moved. For the first time they noticed the sun was already heading down.

"Let's stop before it gets too dark," Thelma said. "I've had such a wonderful time today. I want to remember it forever."

They skated to the riverbank. Lawrence knelt to untie Thelma's skates.

"I'm going to give the boys a skating lesson," he

said. "They're waiting for me."

"See you tomorrow, then. I'll come as early as I can." Thelma disappeared up the trail.

From behind a willow bush, a figure in a dark coat jumped out. Lena ran at Lawrence, her hands lifted in little claws. Without a word, she swiped her fingers at his face. He felt the rasp of her fingernails against his cheek and neck. Then she ran away through the willows.

Leonard rushed over. "You're bleeding," he said. "I'll go tell Mom." He ran off.

Drops of blood fell onto the snow. Lawrence put his hand up to his face. He was bewildered. Why did Lena scratch him? He didn't do anything to her. Now he had to go home and get his cousin Adele to dress the scratches. He untied his skates while John watched in silence.

"I'll teach you tomorrow," Lawrence promised.

Adele cleaned his scratches and put iodine on them. Her husband Frank watched, grinning broadly. "So the girls are fighting over you already," he teased Lawrence. "It must be those CCM skates of yours. Girls love a boy with new CCMs."

So that was it. For the first time, a girl had fought over him. Even though the iodine stung, Lawrence was flattered by the thought.

Chapter 22 ~ The Accident

"D amn, I hate these one-inch boards. They're a headache," Lawrence cussed under his breath. The one-by-four-inch boards slid down the green chain. Not many of that size ever came down, but when they did Lawrence had to pile them in a special place.

Six nights a week Lawrence pulled the lumber off the green chain. As the months passed, he learned to recognize each cut by size and type. The late winter nights weren't as cold now. Spring was coming one of these days.

A piercing whistle blew. The machinery came to a halt. Even so, the lumber kept on sliding down the green chain. An eerie silence filled the early morning air. Lawrence stood still, unsure of what to do. An accident had happened but no matter what, they had to clear the green chain before the next shift. Harold pulled the rest of the lumber off and stacked it. Lawrence pulled a few more pieces of lumber from a pile he had dropped on the walkway.

"That's it for the night," he heard the foreman shout to the workers. "We're a man short. Without a qualified canter, we can't run the sawmill."

When he heard the foreman say canter, Lawrence raced to the lunchroom, his heart beating hard. The foreman caught him by the arm. "James has been hurt. He's in the first aid room. Get over there. He wants to talk to you."

James lay on a stretcher in the first aid room, his face twisted with pain. A first aid man hovered beside him. "He's broken his leg," the man said. "It's already in a splint. We're taking him in the ambulance to the hospital. He wants you to come with us. The foreman says it's okay for you to go."

Lawrence stood back from the stretcher. The room was a cubbyhole, but it had everything needed for an emergency.

Looking at James, Lawrence felt himself go cold. His friend's eyes were closed. "Can he feel anything?" he asked.

"I've given him a painkiller."

James opened his eyes. He tried to smile but it turned into a groan. "I did it this time, didn't I, partner? I broke my leg. I don't know how bad. It's really hurting right now."

"The foreman wants me to go with you to the hospital."

"That's good." James closed his eyes again and rested.

The ambulance ride was a first for Lawrence. He sat in the back with James as it made its silent run along the dark, early-morning road into town.

~

Lawrence was on the way to see James in the hospital. His friend's leg was broken in two places and in a plaster cast that made it seem twice as big. He was already joking with the nurses, smiling his bright friendly smile. He'd make it, Lawrence knew, but it would be a long time before he walked again.

In a small brown bag, Lawrence carried James's shaving gear and a change of clothes. He was lost in thought as he walked the last few blocks to the hospital. He didn't see the sawmill foreman until he was almost passing him.

"Where are you heading?" the foreman asked.

"I'm taking James some stuff from home."

"How's he doing?"

"His leg is smashed up. It still hurts a lot."

The foreman said nothing. Lawrence felt uncomfortable, as if the man was reading his mind. He kicked at a piece of ice underfoot.

"When are you coming back to work?"

Lawrence hesitated. "I'm not. That's it for me."

The foreman shook his head. "You're crazy," he said. "You're the best worker I've had in a long time."

"I don't have a ride to the mill now that James is in the hospital. Anyway, I don't like the green chain."

"I could put you somewhere else."

"That's not it. I'm going travelling."

"You're young, I can see it. I'm still sorry to see you go. You toughed it out all winter when most men would have walked off the green chain."

"I showed you I could do it. I had to prove it to myself, too."

"Yes, you certainly did." The foreman shook his hand. "Take care, Lawrence. Come see me next time if you need a job."

The foreman walked on. 'Now he knows that good things do come in small packages,' Lawrence congratulated himself.

CHAPTER 23 ~ FREEDOM

Winter was almost over and the air was warmer now. Lawrence headed for the skating area. In an hour, the two boys would rush down to the ice. They would be out of breath getting there. Thelma would be close behind.

He wanted time to be alone to think. He sat on a log and set his skates beside him.

Many things had happened since leaving the Mission School. He had grown up and could do a man's job. Working hard made him feel good. 'At least it kept me warm all winter,' he laughed to himself.

The sun felt hot now. He took off his winter jacket to cool down. The wind was soft on his face. There was no one watching his every move anymore. For the first time in his life, it felt good to be alive. Everything was almost perfect. Almost.

Mosoom's words echoed in his mind: "Anger will not get you what you want." Lawrence knew it was true but his anger still came. He sometimes talked sharply to the boys, even to Thelma, the one person who really listened to him. When he did, he felt ashamed and guilty.

'When I first went to the Mission school, I did everything I was told to do,' he remembered. 'As time went on, I didn't want to be good. I tried to break every rule. Mosoom always said that being good is not an easy job. I have to learn to be good again. That's the only way I'm ever going to feel better.'

For the first time, he saw a glimmer of an answer.

He put on his skates and tied them up. He skated slowly at first to warm up. The ice glistened in the afternoon sun. Soon he was far out on the back eddies. His arms and legs worked smoothly together. He started to feel the rhythm of his skating.

He was free to skate when he wanted. He could make his own choices now. He remembered the tea dance with Mosoom, the drumbeats and the singing. He thought of this often and how good it made him feel.

He picked up speed. Elizabeth was going to leave McBride soon and he was going with her. He'd seen the mountains now and knew he would be back one day. Next, he wanted to travel to Europe. It wasn't going to be as easy as getting to McBride. He vowed to make it happen.

A poster on the wall at the train station had given him an idea. It said, "Join the Armed Forces. See the country. See the world."

Maybe...

Epilogue

Goodbye Buffalo Bay is the true story of Larry Loyie's experience in residential school and his return to the world outside. It tells of the emotions children felt when they were taken from their families and shows how other emotions, such as anger, developed. His book honours the friendships that helped children survive. It also shares his adventures, both dramatic and comical, as he enters the working world.

Larry and tens of thousands of other First Nations, Inuit and Métis children experienced harsh treatment at the schools. Poorly funded by the Canadian government, the schools were run by the United, Roman Catholic, Presbyterian and Anglican churches. With little or no professional training, the staff provided inadequate education. Abuse in many forms was common. The children faced constant punishments, ate unhealthy and poorly prepared food, and worked hard at daily chores (such as hauling wood, picking potatoes, washing clothes and sewing) that kept the school running.

Time in the classroom was limited. Teachers and supervisors such as Sister Denise were often not trained to do their jobs. Isolated from their families, the children lived a life of uncertainty and fear. They were constantly told what to do. Above all, they were forbidden to speak their birth language. If they did, they were severely punished by having their mouths washed out with soap, by being beaten and by being ridiculed. Criticism of their families, cultures and languages was a belittling, daily occurrence. An encouraging teacher, such as Sister Theresa, was a one-time experience for the author.

Goodbye Buffalo Bay also explores how a child felt when he or she returned home. Children like Lawrence came home as strangers. Before entering the residential school at nine years of age, he lived a cherished, traditional Cree life and could already provide food for his family by fishing and hunting. After years in the school, he questioned his role at home, in his culture and in the community. The author tells of his struggles and adventures as a teenager as he finds a place for himself in the outside world.

After attending residential school, the majority of children no longer spoke their Indigenous language or valued their culture. This loss helped to widen the divide between family members. Larry's grandmother, Kokom Bella, for example, spoke only Cree. She could no longer talk to most of her grandchildren or teach them traditional ways. Larry refused to forget his language in spite of punishments at the residential school.

A brief history of residential schools

In the 1600s, missionaries ran small schools to teach Indigenous children to act as translators for the fur trade. The first Indian boarding school in Canada— the Mohawk Institute in Brantford, Ontario— opened in 1833 to teach industrial arts. Its daily routine was based on harsh army training.

In 1879, Prime Minister John A. Macdonald of Canada sent journalist Nicholas Flood Davin to visit Carlisle Indian School in Pennsylvania, the first such school in the United States. Davin was impressed. He encouraged Macdonald to support these church-run industrial or manual-labour schools. The name was changed to residential schools in the 1920s.

The goal of the schools was to assimilate Indigenous people into mainstream society, destroying their family and cultural ties. John A. Macdonald told his government that the schools would "do away with a tribal system and assimilate the Indian people in all respects with the inhabitants of the Dominion, as speedily as they are fit to change."

The first of more than 130 schools run by the four church groups (named above) opened in 1892. The schools stressed practical training, such as agriculture and carpentry for boys and sewing and cooking for girls. In 1920, an amendment to the Indian Act made it law for Indigenous parents to send their children to residential school. Parents who resisted could go to jail. In 1949, a Canadian Senate report questioned the residential school system and recommended that the children attend mainstream schools. In 1969, the federal government of Canada assumed responsibility for the schools and began shutting them down. The last of the schools closed in 1998.

On June 11, 2008, Prime Minister Stephen Harper of Canada and the leaders of the Opposition apologized in the House of Commons to the First Nations, Métis and Inuit for the residential schools. The apology was an important step in recognizing the sad history of the residential school system and its long-lasting negative effect on children and families.

Goodbye Buffalo Bay honours the children who attended residential schools and helps to ensure their stories will never be forgotten.

For photographs of Lawrence and other students, the Boys Dormitory, the schoolhouse, the ice rink and activities at residential school, please go to Larry Loyie's website: www.firstnationswriter.com.

Cree Glossary

Kayâs – It's been a long time

Kîkwây eoko? – What is that?

Kimiyosin – You are beautiful

Kokom – Grandmother

Mosoom – Grandfather

Maskwa – bear

Nosîsim – my grandson

Oskiniko – young man

Peyak poko – one only

Tânehki ekâ ka-wîmetawen marbles wayawîtimihk.
– Why aren't you playing marbles outside?

Printed in July 2012
by Gauvin Press,
Gatineau, Québec